THE CAPTIVITY OF THE OATMAN GIRLS

The Shocking History of the Oatman Sisters Massacre

ASHLEY JORDAN

Table of Contents

INTRODUCTION 1

WHO WERE THE OATMANS? 3
    FROM "OUTMAN" TO "OATMAN" 5
    ROYCE OATMAN THE ADULT 7

FROM METHODIST TO MORMON 11
    FROM JOSEPH SMITH TO JAMES COLIN BREWSTER 16

THE OATMAN MASSACRE 44
    THE HEINTZELMAN CONTROVERSY 48
    THE OATMANS CARRY ON 50
    THE DEADLY YAVAPAIS 52

CAPTOR 1 – THE YAVAPAIS TRIBE 60

CAPTOR 2 – THE MOHAVES 72
    THE INFAMOUS MARKINGS 84

ARRIVAL BACK TO CIVILIZATION AND LATER LIFE 88

ACCOUNT 1 – REVEREND ROYAL B. STRATTON 94

ACCOUNT 2 – A. L. KROEBER 98

THE DEATH AND LEGACY OF OLIVE OATMAN 101

INTRODUCTION

Not many people have heard of the name Olive Oatman, yet her story has been an inspiration for books, poems, television shows, and feature films. She was a young girl who experienced horrible tragedies throughout most of her life but put them behind her as a young woman and became the first female public speaker of her time.

Olive Oatman grew up in the early pioneer period of a very young United States of America. She was born in the early 1800s, just a little more than 30 years after the United States gained its independence from Great Britain. Her family lived in the Mideast, which was thriving and secure for white immigrants looking for a better life. The Oatmans moved between Illinois and Pennsylvania, and for the most part enjoyed this area of the world. However, as Mormons, members of the Church of Latter-day Saints, they were tempted to move out West. Little did they know the West was inhabited by Native Americans who harbored animosities towards white men, women, and children. The whites were perceived as taking over the land, something that caused battles between whites and numerous Indian tribes. These hostilities ultimately changed Olive Oatman's life forever.

The Mormon emigration from east to west was a journey that culminated in tragedy for Olive, her parents, and six siblings. The trip was only the beginning for Olive Oatman's heartbreaking young life. Both Olive and her younger sister, Mary Ann, witnessed their family's murder by a pack of savage Indians and were themselves kidnapped. This is the story of the Oatman girls' captivity.

WHO WERE THE OATMANS?

Although the Oatman family's story ended in bloodshed in the Southwest, their narrative began on the other side of North America in Vermont. This is where Olive and Mary Ann's father, Royce Oatman, was born in 1809, where white settlers established fishing and hunting areas in the northeastern woods. It should be noted that the name of Olive and Mary Ann's father is spelled numerous ways in many different writings—Royce, Roys, and Royse. This book uses the first spelling, Royce, although one can say that any of the spellings could be correct, since documents from the past spelled it all three ways.

Royce's family were descendants of Dutch immigrants who traveled during the late 17th century from Holland to western New York. His lineage was traced to a silversmith named Johannes Outman and his wife, Femmetje Kock (also spelled Koch). Outman was born in 1654 in the free city of Hamburg, which was a member of the Hanseatic League and part of the German empire. Outman was documented as being of Dutch descent and raised by a man named Lieve Davits after Outman's parents died. Davits was a gloutlakenwercker, which was another term for a cloth worker.

Johannes Outman moved to Amsterdam, Holland and in 1683 married Royce's mother, Femmetje Kock. Femmetje was the daughter of a silversmith named Yoost Yanss Kock. She was an orphan, raised by a guardian named Roelof Zweeries. The couple had one child while living in Amsterdam named Anna. Outman, his wife, and daughter moved to New York City in 1687, where he worked as a merchant and importer. While there, the couple continued expanding their family.

The Outmans were worshippers at New York's Dutch Reformed Church, which had a large presence in early colonial New York. Numerous leaders of the Dutch war for independence from Spain were members of this church and for a period of time it was the only denomination allowed in New Amsterdam. The descendants of Outman began to migrate to bordering colonies, such as Connecticut and Vermont. Arlington, Vermont, in particular, was the home to Outman's grandson George and his wife, Ruth Wooster. George, along with his son George Jr., fought for the colonists in the American Revolution.

At this point it seemed the family had broken from the Dutch Reformed Church, because George Sr. started to practice Anglican. This religion stemmed from the Protestant Reformation of England in the 16th century. The word itself means "of England," but this connection was less resilient than one would have thought. The Methodist religion swept the area, started by the "father" of Methodism, John Wesley, and his brother Charles. Middletown saw its first Methodist minister in 1801. The new religion spread quickly throughout the area.

From "Outman" to "Oatman"

Royce Oatman's great-grandfather, George Sr., brought the Outman name to the Americas, but it was Royce's grandfather, George Jr., who converted to Methodism and "Americanized" their last name from Outman to Oatman. George Jr.'s brother, Eli, was one of the founders of the Methodist Episcopal Society in the village of Middletown in Rutland County. George Jr. also moved to the village of Middletown and developed the "Oatman Farm" within the forest.

George Jr. married Ann Terrill, and they had three children: Lyman, Eli, and Eliakim. This is where the Outman-turned-Oatman story connects to Olive Oatman. On November 27, 1801 George Jr.'s son, Lyman, married a woman named Lucy Hartland (also of Middletown). The couple had an extremely large family of 12 sons and 5 daughters. The father of Olive Oatman, Royce Oatman, was born in 1809, the fourth child and third son of Lyman and Lucy.

Royce learned at a very young age that religion was an integral part of his upbringing. The Methodist religion in particular became an essential aspect of Royce Oatman's life. As an adult he named his son Lorenzo in honor of a traveling minister who preached in Middletown when Royce was young. Middletown seemed like a safe region for Royce and his family.

They felt secure building their home in Vermont's Rutland County. Although this area was isolated from the more populous areas of New England, it was still safe from one of the biggest and most dangerous threats of white settlers—Indians.

Today Rutland County is the second most populous county in the state of Vermont after Chittenden County (because it houses the city of Burlington), but in the early 19th century this was far from the case. In the early 1800s, the soil was far from fertile, and those who lived in the area had to clear trees and rocks to farm. The weather was also uncomfortable during most of the year, as (like today) the New England region was cold and harsh, even in the summertime. It was not uncommon to have snow in Vermont in June or July, which then destroyed the farmers' crops throughout the summer. These problems became too much for the Oatmans to take. Royce's parents made the decision to move to the town of Locke in western New York to settle a new farm. Western New York was where Royce Oatman enjoyed his young life for some time.

Locke, established in 1802, was located eight miles south of Lake Owasco in western New York. The young Royce Oatman helped work on his family's farm in Locke from morning until night. He was also well-educated. Therefore, Royce was a good mixture of a hard worker on the farm and an educated individual who liked to read books by candlelight. Religion was a strong basis of Locke, with Methodists, Presbyterians, and Baptists preaching vigorously to their congregations. The

Oatmans, committed to their Methodist views, were further inspired by the religious enthusiasm of the Locke region.

For more than a decade the Oatman family lived in Locke and enjoyed the vibrant religious fervor. However, other families started to grow weary of western New York when it seemed the more urban areas did not expand as quickly as they hoped. The Erie Canal officially opened on October 25, 1825, and this completion was supposed to bring new wealth to the area. The canal crossed the Finger Lakes region, 30 miles north of Locke, and spanned 363 miles. It also linked Lake Erie and all the Great Lakes to the Hudson River and New York. Although this completion did help speed up the development of the West, settlers disappointed in the speed of the growth left New York and moved farther west. This exodus out of Locke in the mid-1800s included the Oatman family.

ROYCE OATMAN THE ADULT

In the early 1830s, when Royce was 19, the Oatmans moved to Franklin, which was later named La Harpe, located in Hancock County in western Illinois. This was when Lyman and Lucy built the first hotel in La Harpe and started running a successful business. The Oatman family eventually settled in Illinois, where Lyman and Lucy built a log cabin in Hancock County. They transformed the one-and-a-half story log cabin home into a public inn and took on this new prosperous business through the mid-1800s. In fact, their business thrived so much that they were able to invest in two lots across from their log cabin and built an even larger building called the

Tremont Hotel. When Royce Oatman grew up, Illinois was where he chose to start his own family.

Royce settled in this area of Hancock County, a district that today is still made up of farmers. Farming was the profession Royce moved towards during this time. He purchased land but soon decided to open a store in La Harpe, where his family already built the first hotel of the area. This was where Royce met his future wife. As Royce Oatman got older, he decided where he wanted to live and who he wanted to share his life with. He came to the conclusion that this included a woman named Mary Ann Sperry, the daughter of Joy and Mary Ann Lamont Sperry of Trumbull County, Ohio.

Mary Ann was born on February 11, 1813, had eight siblings, and was the pride of her parents. Her mother was born in New York, while her father was born in Massachusetts. They shared the desire to head west from their eastern homes. In the early 1800s, the Sperry family moved to northeastern Ohio. In 1832 at the age of 23, Royce married Mary Ann at her Mecca, Ohio home. Interestingly enough, this was not the only marriage that bound the Oatmans to the Sperrys; Royce's sisters, Florella and Lorania, both married Mary Ann Sperry's brothers.

Royce and Mary Ann came from reasonably wealthy and well-educated families, so they had a lot in common. The young couple married soon after they first met and lived in La Harpe for two years as farmers before he started a dry goods store. The family lived in Chicago for a year and then moved to rural

Illinois to start a farming family. The newlyweds built a life of farming and tried their hand at the dry goods business before settling in the rural area of Fulton, Illinois.

Soon the Oatmans began building their family with the birth of their first child, Lucy, in August 1834, followed by their son, Lorenzo, in July 1836. Olive Ann Oatman, born on September 7, 1837 in La Harpe, Illinois, was the third child of seven siblings. Four more children followed Olive: Mary Ann, named after her mother, in 1843; Royce Jr. in 1846; Charity Ann in 1848; and Roland in 1859. Royce and Mary Ann soon looked forward to their eighth child, but they never saw its birth.

Overall, the children thought of their father as a cheerful, happy man who had an optimistic viewpoint on life. He was also described as a shorter man, only a little over five feet tall, which was not impressive during that time or today, for that matter. Olive Oatman herself described his appearance as "a medium-sized man, about five feet in height, black hair, with a round face, and yet in the very prime of life". Royce Oatman soon realized, however, that his farm would not be able to support this family of seven (soon to be eight, as Mary Ann again became pregnant).

Royce Oatman came in contact with some relatives who lived in Cumberland County, Pennsylvania. After a few months of preparing his family, they moved to this new area. It only took a few months, however, for Royce Oatman to realize Cumberland County, Pennsylvania was not a suitable region for him or his family. In early 1845 he again packed up his family to head back to Illinois. A year later, in 1846, Mary Ann's sister purchased an adjoining property in Illinois with her husband, Asa Abbott. Mary Ann's parents lived in La Harpe, Illinois but planned to leave their hometown on their own journey out west to join the followers of Mormon leader Brigham Young. Royce and Mary Ann decided to visit them for a week before their trip, but unfortunately, the Sperrys never went on their trek. The couple died, along with their son, Aaron, before they had a chance to leave.

At this point in the life of the Oatman family they had not yet been introduced to the Church of Latter-day Saints. However, Royce Oatman soon was enticed to leave the Methodist religion that was so important to the members of his family who migrated to America. Although Royce was not a follower of the well-known Brigham Young, he became a believer of the religion that changed his life, the Church of Latter-day Saints, also known as the Mormon religion. Olive and her family, who were well-educated and reasonably wealthy, fully practiced the Mormon religion. One might wonder why a man brought up in an enthusiastic Methodist family would turn to the Mormon religion. It was because of the arrival in Hancock County of a charismatic man by the name of Joseph Smith.

From Methodist to Mormon

The Mormon faith is the religion founded by Joseph Smith and the theology of the Latter-day Saint movement. Both the Oatmans and the Sperrys had already heard of Smith, as he was a celebrity because of his self-proclaimed prophet status. The Mormon religion became both the best and worst aspects of the Oatman family. On one hand, Royce and Mary Ann made close friends with other followers and spread the word of their new religion across the area. On the other hand, it tore apart the Oatmans and the Sperrys and was the cause of tragedy for Royce, Mary Ann, and their children. Royce Oatman and his father-in-law, Joy Sperry, got in a nasty verbal battle over who should succeed Joseph Smith after he was killed by gunfire. Royce thought a man by the name of Sidney Rigdon should replace Smith as leader of the Church, while his father-in-law thought Brigham Young was the rightful successor. Rigdon was an anti-polygamist who organized his own church in Pittsburgh, Pennsylvania. However, Joy was set on Rigdon's rival, Brigham Young. Joy and his wife decided to head to Salt Lake City, Utah with 16,000 other Young followers.

Both of these leaders will be discussed later, but there is a reason why this argument about the Mormon leadership is so significant. This is where the disagreement between Royce and his father-in-law illustrated a tragic form of irony for poor Royce. As the two men fought over Rigdon versus Young, Royce Oatman said something very nasty to Joy Sperry that he undoubtedly did not realize was a foreshadowing of his family's own fate: " If you go out west with your family, your children will go hungry, and some will starve to death. Your throats will be cut ear to ear by Indians".

Before Royce and Joy had a chance to fight about Rigdon versus Young, the Church of Latter-day Saints was led by its founder and prophet, Joseph Smith. Smith was born on December 23, 1805 to a commonplace family. His father, Joseph Smith Sr., was a farmer, and his mother, Lucy Mack, came from a family that detached from traditional Congregationalism. She attended Presbyterian meetings, but her husband refused to go and stayed home with his son. These religious differences between his own parents made the young Joseph Smith turn to God for help.

It was seen very early that Smith was special, as he demonstrated astonishing spiritual gifts. At the age of 14 Smith prayed for help and, according to his own account, Jesus appeared to him and told him that all churches were wrong. Then on September 21, 1823 Joseph Smith received another revelation from an angel named Moroni who told him about a set of golden plates that contained a record of ancient inhabitants of America. This angel visited Smith on numerous occasions as the guardian of these golden plates. Smith found them buried in a stone box near his father's farm in western New York on the hill Cumorah. Four years later the angel gave Smith permission to remove them. He was extremely secretive about the stones and kept them locked away in a box. Smith was instructed to translate these stones and, at only 25 years of age, he wrote this translation into a book. Smith's translation became the now infamous *Book of Mormon*. Among other things, this book told the story of a prophet-warrior named after the angel, who buried the golden plates after a battle between two pre-Columbian civilizations. After Moroni died, he became an angel with the specific task of directing only Joseph Smith to the exact location of the golden plates. Joseph Smith found the golden plates and then became the prophet of this religious sect called the "Latter-day Saints." Informally, the Latter-day Saints were known as Mormons.

In March, 1830 Joseph Smith published 5,000 copies of his *Book of Mormon*. There were many individuals who were furious with Smith's *Book of Mormon* and branded his text as blasphemous, yet Royce Oatman was enchanted by Joseph Smith. They were both natives of Vermont; they both came from farming families; and both families went through similar struggles trying to live and prosper in the harsh Vermont weather. What Smith had that Oatman did not, however, was the spiritual gift of talking to Jesus and Moroni. This spirituality that Smith professed was captivating to those who heard about the prophet or had the honor to meet him. Smith founded the Church of Jesus Christ of Latter-day Saints in Fayette, New York, which was only 25 miles from the Oatman farm.

If Royce Oatman truly believed in the *Book of Mormon,* he should probably have taken accounts of the Indians more seriously. The 1830 *Book of Mormon* described Indians in the Nephi Section about two tribes, the Nephites and the Lamanites. In Chapter 5 the Nephites were described as "white, and exceedingly fair, and delightsome", while Chapter 12 describes the Lamanites as "dark, and loathsome, and a filthy people, full of idleness and all manner of abominations". The Nephites' description of the Lamanites definitely resembled that of the Indians. For example, in Enos 1:20 the *Book of Mormon* discusses how the Nephites could not convert the Lamanites to the gospel because of who they had become. Surprisingly, who they were described as becoming (the "bad guys") sounded a lot like a description of Indians: "wild, and ferocious, and a blood-thirsty people, full of idolatry and filthiness; feeding upon beasts of prey; dwelling in tents, and wandering about in the wilderness with a short skin girdle about their loins and their heads shaven; and their skill was in the bow, and in the cimeter, and the ax. And many of them did eat nothing save it was raw meat; and they were continually seeking to destroy us".

It is not clear when Royce Oatman changed from Methodist to Mormon. Mary Ann's brother, Charles Sperry, recollected that Joseph Smith arrived in Hancock County and shortly after, their father joined the Mormon Church during the summer of 1839. It is unclear, however, when the Oatmans joined. Many believe they may not have been associated with the Mormons until more than a year later. This was when a Mormon elder named Zenas Hovey Gurley visited La Harpe. Gurley was a leader in the early Latter-day Saint movement, baptized into the Church on April 1, 1838. He became an elder soon after and was ordained a seventy, a priesthood office within the religion, in 1844. Z. H. Gurley was not always on top of his game with the Latter-day Saint movement. He disagreed with a man named James Strang over the issue of plural marriage and was excommunicated from that church. But in the 1800s Z. H. Gurley made the Mormon religion quite attractive.

When the Oatmans were introduced to the Mormon religion, it was during a time of financial problems. The Oatmans left Hancock County due to these financial struggles and moved back to La Harpe in western Illinois when things did not get any better. The La Harpe community renewed its commitment to the Mormon religion, but the sect did have its detractors. Many people in Illinois and across the United States found the Church of Latter-day Saints to be offensive, starting with its leader, Joseph Smith.

These detractors, however, did not stop the Mormon religion from spreading through Illinois and other states across the east. In March 1841 the Mormon Church's official Nauvoo, Illinois newspaper, the *Times and Seasons,* reported that Z. H. Gurley would be baptizing 52 La Harpe residents. This newspaper was the official 19th-century publication of the Latter-day Saints and was printed monthly or twice-monthly from November 1839 through February 1846. During that time it was the main publication that spread information about the religion. The Mormon religion flourished throughout Hancock County, and the communication between La Harpe, which housed the Oatmans, and Nauvoo grew stronger over time. It was also attractive to a family like the Oatmans who were looking for something positive during a darker financial time.

From Joseph Smith to James Colin Brewster

Joseph Smith moved the headquarters of his Church of Latter-day Saints to Kirtland, Ohio. This was where Smith also founded the first Mormon-controlled bank, but it went out of business during the national Panic of 1837. This financial crisis was the beginning of a national depression that lasted through the mid-1840s. This economic downturn caused Smith's bank to go bankrupt and drove Smith and the Mormons out of the area. In fact, Smith was forced to flee Kirtland or be criminally prosecuted by those who made claims that he had mismanaged their financial investments. He and his followers escaped to Missouri, but rumors of polygamy (rumors that still plague the religion today) forced them to run again. Other mishaps followed, as it seemed the Mormons attracted opposition wherever they moved and tried to start fresh.

Tensions continued to build between the Latter-day Saints and the other American settlers to the point that it cost their prophet's life. While Joseph Smith was imprisoned in Carthage,

Illinois, he was murdered by a mob on June 27, 1844. Two hundred state militiamen were transformed into an anti-Mormon mob and fired rifle shots into the cell of Smith and his brother, Hyrum. The two brothers were killed instantly. Many followers thought the Mormon religion would die along with Smith, but his successor, Brigham Young, revitalized the religion and moved the group out west. However, Young had opposition before he became the successor to Joseph Smith. This fight for control of the Church of Latter-day Saints connected to the fight between Royce Oatman and his father-in-law.

Joseph Smith was only 38 years old when he was killed. The prophet was too young to have named a successor to the church's highest leadership role. Sidney Rigdon was the only surviving member of the church's three-president First Presidency. Immediately Rigdon claimed that he had the right to be the church's guardian. Rigdon reportedly received visions along with Smith, but he was later admonished by his once visionary counterpart. In fact, he was tarred and feathered with Smith and later fell into a depression. However, when Smith organized the church's First Presidency, he made Rigdon and Jess Gause his first two counselors. Smith later tried to replace Rigdon in 1843 by accusing him of various crimes.

The congregation voted to allow Rigdon to keep his position, and although Smith continued to be wary of Rigdon, he actually chose him to be his vice-presidential running mate when Smith ran for president of the United States. Yes, believe it or not, Joseph Smith and Sidney Rigdon ran for president and vice president of the United States in 1844. The United States presidential election was scheduled for November of that year, but Smith was killed on June 27th. An unknown man, James K. Polk, beat the much more well-known Whig party candidate, Henry Clay, and was elected the 11th President of the United States on November 5, 1844. One may wonder what would have happened in this election if Joseph Smith lived until the November 5th election. However, he did not, and this left not only the United States presidency open for a dark horse like Polk but also the leadership of the Church of Latter-day Saints.

Sidney Rigdon had a few challengers to the Latter-day Saint throne. One was a recent convert to Mormonism named James Jesse Strang. Strang was from Voree, Wisconsin and claimed that he was appointed to be the successor of Joseph Smith as the leader of the Church of Jesus Christ of Latter-day Saints. He testified to having a letter from Smith that named him as successor. Strang urged Rigdon and another candidate, Brigham Young, not to leave their current positions so that he could take on the leadership role left by Smith. However, both Rigdon and Strang lost to a carpenter turned president of the Quorum of the Twelve Apostles named Brigham Young.

How did Brigham Young become the second president of the Church of Jesus Christ of Latter-day Saints over both Rigdon and Strang? Both Rigdon and Strang had impressive résumés within the church, probably more impressive than Young. It was said that Joseph Smith recorded a revelation he had that specified how the church should be led by the Quorum of the Twelve Apostles. Therefore, it was easy for Young, who had a direct connection to the Quorum of the Twelve Apostles, to claim that the leadership of the church now fell to them. In addition, many of his followers claimed that when Young made his case to the congregation, he resembled and sounded exactly like Joseph Smith. So, three and a half years after the murder of Joseph Smith, Brigham Young became President of the Church of Jesus Christ of Latter-day Saints.

Brigham Young, William E. McLellin, and other church leaders continued to build the Mormon religion after the tragic death of their prophet. However, Royce Oatman was not sure about the Quorum of the Twelve Apostles now being the church's single most governing body. There were disputes in his hometown of La Harpe between the three highest ranking men—Rigdon, Strang, and Young—about who should succeed Joseph Smith. There was also no consensus among the followers. As discussed earlier, this disagreement reached the Oatman family when Royce's father-in-law was certain that Young's Quorum of the Twelve Apostles should be the church's governing body going forward. However, Oatman did not share his father-in-law's viewpoint. Oatman was more confident about Sidney Rigdon.

In the fall of 1845, Royce Oatman had a meeting with one of Rigdon's missionaries and was quickly impressed with how he presented Rigdon's view of the church. Oatman was so impressed that he moved his wife and children east to south-central Pennsylvania where Rigdon's "Adventure Farm" was located. Rigdon announced at the General Conference in

Philadelphia that he planned to re-establish this community near the small town of Greencastle, Pennsylvania.

Rigdon made remarkable claims that this "quiet village of Greencastle" would "become the glory of the whole earth". However, once the Oatmans were fully assimilated into Rigdon's flock, they soon realized his leadership was angry and difficult at best, frightening and enraged at worst. The Oatmans decided to leave Rigdon and return to Illinois. They moved to Whiteside County just east of the Mississippi River in the town of Fulton. This is where they built their log cabin and spent a happy and fruitful time as a family.

Illinois continued to be the hub for the Mormon religion. Sidney Rigdon was excommunicated from the church and, in Springfield, Illinois, Hazen Aldrich was chosen to be the organization's first president. This is when he elected two men, James Colin Brewster and James Goodale, as his counselors. There was no way for McLellin to know that James C. Brewster would become integral in a division within the Mormon faith and the downfall to the Oatman family.

Brewster was born around 1826 or 1827 in Buffalo, New York to Zephaniah and Jane, who converted to Mormonism and joined the Latter-day Saints in Kirtland, Ohio. His father was a carpenter who helped other Mormons build Joseph Smith's first temple. This is probably when the young Brewster (only around 10 years old) caught the eye of Joseph Smith. Some Mormons claimed that this young man had a gift for "seeing in vision distant objects not seen by the natural eye".

The young Brewster was soon invited to meet Joseph Smith's father, Joseph Smith Sr., along with two other men, Elders Beaman and Holman. It was documented in the first volume of the *Olive Branch* that the three men put their hands on the head of the young Brewster and claimed that he was "a prophet, a seer, a revelator and translator" and that he "should have power given me of God to discover and obtain the treasures which are hid in the earth".

In 1837, at the young age of 11, Brewster professed that he had received a divine notification, a direct contact from God, that declared him to be the head of the Mormon Church. Now, the Mormon faith believed only Joseph Smith could translate God's will. As discussed, Smith had multiple connections with the divine faith, which encouraged him to create the *Book of Mormon* and the Mormon religion. Therefore, Brewster's claims created a split among Mormon followers. One of the followers of Brewster was Royce Oatman.

Joseph Smith, however, was not impressed with the fact that this young boy had a powerful vision. In fact, he was annoyed that James C. Brewster said he had a vision at all. Smith was adamant that the Mormon religion specified that only he could channel God. Second, Brewster was against polygamy, which probably angered Smith, since he had nearly 40 wives. Some of Smith's wives were already married to other men, and one was rumored to be only 14 years old. For Smith's first wife, Emma, the polygamy was excruciating, even though Smith did not have sex with all of his wives. Smith was not alone in his support of polygamy. His successor, Brigham Young, had an astounding

55 wives, and 16 of them bore him 59 children by the time he died in 1877. Brewster, on the other hand, set himself apart by having a strict loyalty to the concept of monogamy—one husband, one wife.

The late 1830s were already a tumultuous time for the Latter-day Saints. As mentioned earlier, the Panic of 1837 affected not only their Kirtland church but half of the banking institutions all over the country. The five-year long economic depression greatly hurt the Latter-day Saint followers, including the Oatmans. Brigham Young also had problems in Illinois. The local media made a case against the group. Attempting to finish Smith's lavish temple during this time was all but impossible. More violence ensued between the Mormons and the non-Mormons. Therefore, when Brewster started to make his assertions of a better life elsewhere, these declarations were tempting to Royce Oatman.

The Oatmans firmly rejected the likes of Rigdon, Strang, and Young. So, they were susceptible to a new leader when Brewster came on the scene. Brewster asserted that he wrote one of the books of Esdras, which was impressive in of itself. What made these assertions more impressive was that they were made by a very young man who still lived with his mother and father in Springfield, Illinois.

In 1838 young James Colin Brewster claimed he had a vision that he was to write the lost books of Esdras. At that time he was too young, only around 12 years old, to write these clearly and comprehensively. However, soon after this pronouncement he began to write the books. By 1842 Brewster finished his book. In these writings Brewster claimed there was a "Land of Bashan" out towards California.

Joseph Smith was warned about this young man who had supposedly written these books of Esdras, and at one point Smith promised to read them. Smith did not communicate, however, to the young prophet about his writings. Brewster's writings stated there was an ancient Hebrew prophet who predicted the end of the world in 1878. But what probably angered Smith more was that Brewster predicted the reorganization of the Church under Brewster's leadership. The Church denounced Brewster in its official publication *Times and Seasons* on page 24 of its December 1842 edition: "We have lately seen a pamphlet, written and published by James C. Brewster; purporting to be one of the lost books of Esdras; and to be written by the gift and power of God. We consider it a perfect humbug, and should not have noticed it, had it not been assiduously circulated, in several branches of the church". Brewster claimed his book of Esdras declared the area along the Colorado River as the Promised Land for his followers. Joseph Smith was later killed, and the Latter-day Saints then sought a new leader. For many, including the Oatmans, that leader was James C. Brewster.

Brewster and fellow Latter-day Saint movement leader Hazen Aldrich founded the Church of Christ. This movement was a sect of the Latter-day Saints, and Brewster claimed it was the true successor to John Smith's original Church of Christ he founded in 1830. However, Brewster disagreed with and verbally attacked the leadership of The Church of Jesus Christ of Latter-day Saints who were located in the home base of Salt Lake City, Utah. These disagreements triggered Brewster to break from the followers of the second president of the Church, Brigham Young, who founded Salt Lake City and served as the first governor of the Utah Territory. Despite Young's power within the church, Brewster turned against him and his followers.

Meanwhile, Brewster claimed that he continued to receive revelations from God. His promises of a paradise in the valleys of the Colorado and Gilda Rivers were tempting to many of the Mormons, including Royce Oatman. His followers, called the "Brewsterites," were then born. Brewster's assurances of a better life for the Mormons could not have come at a more opportune time. Life for the Mormons was not easy. The winters were devastating both physically and economically. The Panic of 1837 did not help, either.

In the spring of 1848 Brewster published a pamphlet that included the 11th Book of Esdras titled *An Address to the Church of Christ, and Latter Day Saints.* That same year he joined Hazen Aldrich, another early leader of the Latter-day Saints movement, to found the Church of Christ. Young and Strang condemned this church as apostasy, an abandonment of their religious beliefs. These allegations did not phase Brewster or Aldrich, and the two men continued to claim that their church was the true successor of Smith's Church of Christ originally founded 18 years before. As noted earlier, Aldrich was selected as the sect's first president after the death of Smith.

He chose Brewster and Goodale as the First President's counselors.

Under Aldrich's reign, Brewster and Goodale started a newspaper called the *Olive Branch*, which disseminated many of Brewster's own revelations. Brewster used this newspaper to publicize his teachings and criticisms of the Mormon church led by Joseph Smith. Smith organized his own migration of followers to Salt Lake City, Utah and stated this would be the true home of the Mormon people. The fact that the Salt Lake City Mormons who followed Smith thrived angered Brewster. The *Olive Branch* was a great way to get Brewster's points across for the Mormons. He tried to lure Young's followers away by publishing letters in the *Olive Branch* from newly converted Brewsterites who, instead of following Young to Salt Lake City, Utah, chose to follow Brewster to Bashan.

The January 1849 issue of the *Olive Branch* announced plans to arrive at the Land of Bashan by the end of 1851. Brewster also made a very dangerous claim that the natives were friendly, a promise that was broken in disastrous terms for the Oatmans: "The bottoms of the Colorado and the Gila, with their tributaries, are broad, rich and well timbered. Every thing in the shape of vegetation attains a lusty size, amply evincing the exuberant fecundity of the soil producing it. There are many sweet spots in the vicinity of both these streams, well deserving the name of earthly Eden. Man here might fare sumptuously, with one continual feast spread before him...*The natives, for the most part, may be considered friendly, or at least not dangerous*". The last part of Brewster's writing is key to the

Oatmans' downfall, as they must have believed their new prophet about the friendliness of the natives.

Royce Oatman and others were blinded by Brewster's description of Bashan, the so-called new Promised Land. Brewster planned exactly how Bashan would be designed for his followers. He intended Bashan to resemble its own small state, with blocks and small towns forming different townships. He directed his Brewsterites how they should pack for their trip so they could be prepared for their journey to Bashan. According to their prophet, they each needed two wagons, which were pulled by oxen. Clothes for an entire year were to be brought so that both summer and winter were planned for, while farming equipment was to cover two years. He also recommended how much food everyone should bring—a pound per day of flour, rice, and beans for each person. He recommended the followers not pack any meat but instead suggested firearms for hunting along their travels. Brewster went so far as to recommend reading materials that covered science and history, only nonfiction texts.

On June 23, 1849 the group held its General Assembly in the Kirtland Temple in Kirtland, Ohio. It was here that six members of the group agreed with Brewster's election to move to California, which Brewster asserted was the "intended place of gathering" for the Mormon faith. During the summer of the same year the father of 11-year-old Olive Ann Oatman decided to relocate his family in the name of their religion and in search of prosperity. In February 1850 an announcement was published in the *Olive Branch* about a Brewsterite who decided to obtain his family's ticket to Bashan. This announcement was made by Royce Oatman. By December 1849 Royce Oatman had formally decided to join the Brewsterites. Royce Oatman wasted no time selling his farm in Whiteside County for $1,000 and some personal property for another $500. He officially closed his business and packed up his family for their long trek out west to the Promised Land.

Brewster promised that any followers ("saints") who followed him to this Promised Land would be rewarded generously with a "life of peace and plenty". According to Brewster this Promised Land, along the Colorado and Gilda Rivers, was fertile for growth, wooded for protection, and mild in climate. He also assured his followers that the Native Americans who lived there were welcoming. As he wrote in his publication, they were friendly and not dangerous. Royce Oatman also did not question Brewster's claims and was sold on the trip.

The Oatmans were part of the Brewsterites, a group that was appropriately named after their prophet. Now, these Brewsterites were not alone in the quest for prosperity out west; in fact, around a quarter of a million Americans made the long, tough journey west between 1849 and 1853. The *Olive Branch* moved to Brewster's home state of Illinois and published in October 1849 that the group planned to move from Illinois to California.

Oatman in particular was enticed by this promise of fertile land in California, where his family would be safe and free. In addition, he was also told there was a potential to mine gold and silver, made accessible by the American government. For a man with seven children and an eighth on the way, it seemed like a no-brainer to pack up his family and head off with the Brewsterites. However, Oatman did not realize that the claims made by Brewster were false. In fact, Brewster's claims in the *Olive Branch* reported a deadly piece of misinformation: "The natives, for the most part, may be considered friendly, or, at least, not dangerous. Some of them, in the neighborhood of the Gila and the Gulf of California, are partially advanced and civilized, and cultivate the ground, raising corn, melons, pumpkins, beans, potatoes... The conditioning character of these tribes present most flattering inducements for missionary enterprise, and should efforts for their amelioration be put forth by a zealous and devoted man, a glorious fruition of their most sanguine hopes might soon be expected".

Brewster, whose occupation was listed as "Mormon Prophet," professed there was a land of opportunity called "Bashan" in the Rio Grande Valley, which was a region located in south Texas and northern Mexico. In search of both gold and God, Brewster claimed that God had selected this region to be the new gathering location for the Latter-day Saints. It was finally time for Brewster and Goodale to lead a wagon train of followers to "Bashan." Aldrich stayed in Kirtland and continued his work there, as he had begun to doubt the prophetic abilities of Brewster.

Brewster continued to use his publication, the *Olive Branch*, as a means to lure the Brewsterites towards the Promised Land of Bashan. He told them to plan for at least six months of travel, a gross underestimate. His followers were encouraged to pack up their cows and young cattle, wagons, and farm tools. The plan was set for the group of followers to find a new life of prosperity out west. Royce Oatman also became a spokesperson for Brewster who traveled around Illinois during February 1850 to spread the gospel of Brewster's Books of Esdras along with the *Book of Mormon*. Oatman claimed he converted four former Mormons to the Brewsterites.

The Oatmans left their home in Whiteside County on Monday, May 6, 1850 and headed to meet the rest of the Brewsterites in Independence, Missouri. This is where the group organized a wagon train in the name of their prophet, the one and only James Colin Brewster. The Oatmans were finally on their way to make the long journey to Bashan, which promised prosperity for their growing family. Royce, Mary Ann, and the children first headed west, crossed the Mississippi River by ferry, and then started south towards Missouri. They were joined by another family, the Meteeres, in a village called West Buffalo, Iowa. George Meteere, a church elder, helped organize Brewster's church in Springfield, Illinois and later became an elder of the West Buffalo branch. Now that the Oatmans had more Brewsterites on their journey, they traveled until they joined the Thompsons of Moscow. Ira W. Thompson made the trip with his wife and four children. Together they continued towards the next stop in Independence.

Thirteen-year-old Olive Oatman was excited about her family's upcoming adventure. They headed across the

Mississippi River to join the Brewsterites in Independence, Missouri in late June. Independence was a common place for families to meet before traveling together to new destinations. Their time in Independence was spent purchasing needed supplies and coordinating with the other families on the trip. From guns and ammunition to farm tools and water kegs, the Oatmans were set to head out west with their companions. However, the Brewsterites began to show their frustration as they waited throughout the hot summer month of July to get moving. When the Brewsterites were finally gathered together, they realized they still needed more supplies and took time in Independence to acquire them.

The Oatmans bought supplies needed for their two wagons. They gathered food, weapons, and water. They also purchased cattle which would provide fresh milk during their voyage. Their faith took them across the country on a journey from Missouri to California. However, they never reached their destination. The group, which included wagons and heads of cattle, traveled from the Missouri range to find the Bashan. They were supplied with guidebooks that claimed their journey would be easy and quick, three to four months tops. Of course, this claim was far from reality. These trips typically took nearly a year to complete, and since the families did not plan for this amount of time, they were close to starvation when they reached California, if they did not die en route.

By July 15th the Brewsterites had elected James Goodale as the captain to lead them to their destiny. Goodale and Brewster were the first counselors of their friend Hazen Aldrich's First

Presidency. Although Goodale definitely had the pedigree for leadership, Brewster worried about the discontent forming within his Brewsterites. The trip was already running late, and numerous families depended on Brewster to lead them to safety out west. Brewster himself traveled with his parents and five siblings. Tensions continued to rise as one family grumbled about having to share their supplies, while another pioneer turned back.

When they were only about 20 miles west of Independence in late July, some of the travelers voiced their dissatisfaction with their group. Some of these detractors still believed in Brewster's Books of Esdras and the journey to Bashan, but they no longer wanted to travel to their Promised Land with the current Brewsterites. Some of these critics broke from the group and grew distant from the other families. They refused to share their supplies with others and continued to withdraw. By the end of July their expedition to paradise had barely begun, yet Brewster saw trouble. He wrote in the *Olive Branch*: "During the last two weeks, all that the power of Satan and the iniquity of the ungodly could accomplish, has been done to produce discord and division among us; and in several instances they came well-nigh accomplishing their object, but the saints overcome. Throughout this time the majority of the company have stood firm and united, and have manifested by their conduct under the most trying circumstances, that they believe the word of God".

The Brewsterites finally set off for paradise on August 9, 1850, a month behind schedule. That being said, Olive described the night before they left as lovely when the group convened in Independence. Migrating from east to west was not a foreign thought process during this time. In fact, a quarter of a million Americans emigrated west between 1849 and 1853.

On August 10, 1850, a bright and sunny Friday afternoon, approximately 43 wagons with 90 Brewsterites—men, women, and children—left Independence down the Santa Fe Trail to prosperity. The children in particular were happy and excited about the trip. They were more than likely unaware of their parents' discontent. The children of the Brewsterites did not have a worry in the world—not about lack of food, not about getting sick, not about disease, and certainly not about running into dangerous Indians. As one of the older children, Olive probably thought the same thing. She later wrote about her recollections of that time: "How little we thought what was before us".

The Santa Fe Trail was the largest supply route that connected Independence and Santa Fe. Wagons, cattle, and families chatted and laughed, many total strangers before that day. The Oatmans were one of the largest families in the group. The travelers owned more than 20 wagons and hundreds of cattle. Oatman was offered $250 for his two horses by one of his fellow pioneers, and James Brewster himself encouraged him to accept the offer. But Royce Oatman refused, as horses were not as efficient as oxen to pull his family's wagon.

The Brewsterites were now more than a month behind their initial departure date. Leaving in August was not ideal, as pioneers who successfully made the trip to California previously suggested they leave months earlier due to the weather. May or June at the latest was recommended so the weather would be optimal for the health and welfare of the families. When the Brewsterites finally set off in August, the travelers had no idea what was in store for them. It was so hot during this time that the grass was already brown, and water was scarce. Once some of the travelers came to the realization that the hot summer weather was not ideal for traveling out west, resentment set in.

The hot summer sun also made the travel unbearable even when protected in the shade of the wagons. The wagons themselves reached an unbearable 110 degrees during the day. At night the families slept in crowded tents or crude, provisional beds under wagons if the tents were drenched from storms. That being said, the Oatman family was initially pleased with their progress. Duties were divided by gender. The women baked and did the laundry, while the men hunted and fished. The children played games with each other, danced to music, and told stories around the campfire. Breakfast consisted of pancakes, fried meat, and tea or coffee before the adults got the wagons ready for the next leg of the journey. The families worked together harmoniously at first and got to know each other very well. However, the hot weather, the monotony of travel, and several misfortunes made some of the families question whether or not they made the right decision to follow Brewster to paradise.

For example, at one point during the trip, three-year-old Roland fell off the wagon and nearly died when a wheel ran over his neck. His father wrote about it in the *Olive Branch:* "I took him up, and saw that he was about to depart this life...but not feeling willing to part with him, I administered to the child according to the law and order of the gospel, and the Lord Blessed him, and he soon recovered, and is now hearty and well". A young girl was not so lucky, as 19-year-old Mary Lane died of tuberculous on September 16th. Each family donated a board from their wagon so the family could build a casket for her.

Mary Lane's father, Asa, died two months later in November, also more than likely from tuberculous. Olive remembered Asa Lane as "a man of stern integrity, appreciated and loved by us all, and his death was an irreparable loss". However, the group was no longer able to make a casket. Instead, they simply covered his body with a blanket and buried him in a grave. The only thing that marked the spot of his burial was a wooden stake which displayed his name. His daughter, Isabel, was left all alone, her father and sister both taken from her as she traveled to what she thought was a Promised Land. Worse still were the living conditions. Disease was always a worry, since the travelers used the same water for drinking, bathing, and waste. It was disgusting.

Any camaraderie between the adults did not last. About 100 miles into their travels, fights began. First, their leader, Charles Brewster, turned into an unpleasant and disagreeable fanatic. For example, he was more than likely questioned when, seemingly out of nowhere, he changed his mind about his revelation that the Promised Land was along the Colorado

River. He claimed a new revelation revealed that it was near the Rio Grande. The Rio Grande just happened to be 600 miles closer than the Colorado River. Other religious disagreements started to spring up among his followers, as well. Those squabbles, coupled with the wearisomeness of the constant travel and anxieties about the threat of Indians, made the group start to implode.

At this point, some of the families started to threaten to return to Independence, Missouri instead of continuing on to the Promised Land of Bashan. The other families ultimately persuaded them to stay, but this did not help quell the resentment within the once tight-knit group. In addition to the resentment, disagreements between Brewster and Goodale divided the group as they reached Santa Fe in the New Mexico Territory. Some of the followers had already questioned Brewster's leadership skills and soon realized he was not the charismatic and alluring leader like his predecessors, Joseph Smith and Brigham Young. Most of Brewster's followers abandoned the prophet, and these deserters included the Oatman family. The Oatmans left their Illinois farm in May of that year and then joined 20 other families in July. Those families and others stuck together, even with all of the infighting, to protect themselves from one threat—Indians.

Texas settlers were known to have forced many Comanches and Kiowas out of the state, which made Indians destructive predominantly along the Santa Fe Trail. The Comanches were a North American Indian tribe with a name that literally means "anyone who wants to fight me all the time". They were originally part of the Wyoming Shoshone but moved south towards Texas and New Mexico after they successfully attacked and displaced other tribes, such as the horribly malicious Apaches. By the 1800s, when the Oatmans and crew traveled through the southwest, the Comanches were very powerful and dangerous. There may have been anywhere from 7,000 to 30,000 members, and in 1864 United States forces led an unsuccessful campaign against the Comanches.

The Kiowas, the other tribe that frequented the area in the southwest, migrated from the upper north area of the United States (now southwestern Montana) into the Great Plains at some point in the 18th century. They were accompanied by a small southern Apache band known as the Kiowa Apache. They eventually formed a lifelong peace with the Comanches and other Indian tribes. They shared a reservation with the Comanches and were deadly fighters. In fact, the Kiowa men achieved rank by their feats during war, such as killing enemies. The white pioneers, including Royce Oatman, knew that Indians were their biggest threat. However, as the group continued into the New Mexico Territory, the leadership began to break down and threaten the group's unity one last time.

Royce Oatman and Ira Thompson wanted James Goodale to be removed as captain of the group. When he was not removed, they simply stopped listening to him. Brewster eventually demoted Goodale and replaced him with Royce Oatman. Royce's appointment was the final straw for the group when he went head-to-head with Brewster. Brewster wanted to take a difficult side trip to Santa Fe to get his mail, but Royce was against it. He wanted the group to continue on the much faster southern route. This final bickering resulted in the group parting ways. On October 9th, about 30 people followed Brewster towards Santa Fe. They bought land in Socorro (New Mexico) and named their new settlement after a prophet in the writings of Esdras named "Colonia." The other 50 or so, which included the original families who traveled with the Oatmans, the Thompsons, and the Meteeres, elected Royce Oatman as their captain and continued their trip west to Bashan. Oatman's group met with these Brewsterites briefly in Socorro in November, but Brewster was no longer a welcoming prophet. He wrote in his *Olive Branch* that Oatman's crew had "gained the reputation of being the most dishonest men that had ever been in the country". The Oatman crew made money at an army post cutting and gathering hay before leaving the Brewsterites and continuing on their way.

Those who followed Brewster were in for an unwelcoming surprise. Their journey proved difficult, from snowstorms and droughts to disease and death, yet Brewster finally took those who remained to his promised land along the Colorado River. However, it was not the Bashan he described in the *Olive Branch*, "a land of hills, of [valleys], of plains and pleasant places, which brings forth in abundance, that they who go there shall prosper". The Bashan Brewster brought the small group of followers to was a wasteland. It was noted that Brewster himself did not stay in his so-called paradise of Bashan. Brewster reportedly traveled to California, but he actually returned to Litchfield, Illinois with his family.

Meanwhile, eight of the wagons followed their new leader, 42-year-old Royce Oatman, down the Rio Grande-Gila route. This new group, minus their prophetic leader, headed to California by way of the southern route through Socorro, New Mexico and Tucson, Arizona. Oatman was a merciless leader who did not like to follow orders and was very stubborn. Once Royce Oatman made up his mind about something, it seemed he would rather suffer a misfortune than back down or admit he was wrong. This stubbornness meant Oatman rode the group for long periods of time in the oppressive heat through treacherous terrain. Due to this trait, it was probably not a surprise that Royce Oatman was labeled as the main troublemaker of the group. A man by the name of Max Greene described him as "sinfully reckless," "a most dangerous companion on the Grand Prairie," and "the nucleus of our troubles". He sarcastically stated that if the group could have exchanged Royce Oatman for smallpox, they probably would have.

Royce Oatman did not remain captain for long. He was replaced by a man named Norman C. Brimhall after Oatman complained that two of his horses were stolen due to poor guarding. In reality, they were stolen by Indians and later sold to Mexicans. Regardless, Royce was no longer in charge. The group, led by Brimhall, continued west on Col. Philip St. George Cooke's 1846 route. However, the month of November proved to be difficult. At first it was because of the rough, mountainous roads, and then three inches of snow. Luckily, the group had a bit of good luck when, after being without water for an entire day, they found water to drink, timber for firewood, and turkey, wild sheep, deer, and antelope for food. It was just the break the group needed after the rough, disheartening travels they endured as the weather got colder. The Oatman family was packed into two wagons.

The group was regularly approached by Indians and fearful for their lives at every turn. The women tried to satisfy and calm them by giving them cooked beans, but when three Apaches entered the camp, the pioneers knew they were trouble. The Apaches acted friendly toward the group, and that alone was suspicious, but the group also knew the dangerous history between the Apaches and whites. That night the group's dogs gave them nonstop warnings. Were the dogs correct with their suspicions? Yes. The next morning Royce and the others awoke to a dozen of their animals missing and Indian tracks around their campsite. At this point the Oatmans had no cattle to tow their wagons and were forced to leave everything behind. Without their wagons the Oatmans continued along the San Pedro River with the others. They finally made it to Santa Cruz, a walled city protected by 50 Mexican troops because it was frequently attacked by Indians. The area had just been raided by the dreaded Apaches. So, the pioneers headed onward to what they hoped was a much safer refuge away from the dangers of the Apaches and other treacherous Indian tribes. Things for the pioneers turned from bad to worse. By now Royce doled out just one and a half dry biscuits a day per person.

More than 100 miles into their trip, the group finally arrived in Tucson, Arizona on January 8, 1851, but they were in desperate need of supplies. Their food situation was grim, and the lack of rainfall over the winter months made it all but impossible to find necessities. The Mexicans were there celebrating the Feast of Epiphany, a Christian holiday that celebrates the visit to baby Jesus by the magi and Jesus' baptism by John the Baptist. It is one of the three oldest festival days of the Christian church and in Tucson was celebrated with firecrackers, dancing, and eating.

Some of the travelers decided to remain in Tucson until they could acquire much-needed supplies. This group of families spent nearly a month in Tucson before separating again. One of the women who stayed, the wife of Ira Thompson, said that "luck favored us" and explained that, although they were the first white women to arrive in the village and there may have been bad blood after the Mexican-American War, a poultice she made out of sugar, soap, and the white of an egg for an elderly Mexican's foot won them over. The Thompsons and four other families decided to stay in Tucson to wait for help. Royce was not one of them. He and two other families, the Kellys and the Widlers, insisted on continuing another 45 miles to Maricopa Wells.

As the Oatmans and other families reached Socorro and Tucson, Royce Oatman took control of the travelers. Under Oatman's command the group reached the New Mexico Territory in 1851. They looked for an adequate area to build their camp and rest for the night. However, they soon realized the New

Mexico climate was unfit for their living needs. The other families steadily deserted the group's objective of trying to reach the mouth of the Colorado River. With more than 200 miles left to travel just to reach the banks of the Colorado River, the group stopped in Maricopa Wells, Arizona. This is where they were warned about the dangers of the Native Americans.

As the group continued west towards Maricopa Wells, located in the northern part of the Mexican state of Sonora, they knew that some welcoming Indian tribes existed. The families traveled with the hope of running into the friendly Pima and Maricopa tribes. Maricopa Wells, located in Pinal County, Arizona, was historically a frequent stop for travelers of the southwest route between Texas and California. The Oatmans, Kellys, and Widlers arrived there on February 5th and found nearly 1,000 starving Indians. At this point, Mary Ann Oatman was only weeks away from giving birth to her eighth child.

The Pimas and the Maricopas were well-known as the two Indian tribes that lived in villages along the Gila River. They were friendly to whites as well as to each other and, similar to the three white families, these Indians were also fearful of being attacked by the dreadful Apaches. The Pimas were North American Indians who lived along the Gila and Salt Rivers, and the Gila was the waterway the Oatmans needed to cross to get to California. This tribe was literally called the "River People" as they were split between the Gila River Indian community and the Salt River Pima-Maricopa Indian community. The Pimas were mostly farmers. They were not known as hunters for sport, only necessity.

The Maricopas lived alongside the Pimas beside the Gila and Salt Rivers within the two communities mentioned above. The Maricopas, however, did not escape attack. In 1825 an American frontiersman named James Ohio Pattie led an attack on the Maricopa Tribe and slaughtered 200 of them in revenge for a previous attack. The Maricopas formed a confederation with the Pimas. Both the Kellys and the Widlers planned to stay in Maricopa Falls for a week, and they strongly recommended that the Oatmans follow suit. Royce Oatman's plan was to continue with his family along the Gila and Colorado Rivers, but everyone knew how dangerous that area was both for warring Indians and the treacherous land. However, these fears did not deter Royce Oatman. He and his family had already traveled more than 1,000 miles, and only a few hundred remained.

The other families knew this area declined in 1850 after a former scalp hunter and leader of the notorious Glanton Gang named John Glanton apprehended a ferry service at the Yuma Crossing operated by an Indian tribe called the Quechans (then called the Yumas) in the "Glanton Massacre." Glanton was one of the early settlers of Mexican Texas and, along with his Glanton Gang, became a mercenary after the Mexican-American War in the American southwest. In 1849 Glanton and his followers killed bands of Apache Indians in Northern Mexico. They also murdered and scalped peaceful American Indians and Mexican citizens. Glanton and his group were partners in a ferry at Yuma Crossing. The Glanton Massacre occurred after Glanton and his men destroyed the Quechans' boat and killed some of the Quechans who were operating the rival ferry. On April 23, 1850 the Quechans, led by Caballo en Pelo, killed and scalped Glanton and most of his gang. This retaliation led to the Gila Expedition, an 1850 California militia attack on the Quechan tribe. It was California's first military operation against aboriginal Americans.

Royce talked to an entomologist named John Lawrence LeConte, who recently traveled from Fort Yuma to Maricopa Wells. LeConte claimed he had absolutely no trouble with Indians along that route. Royce Oatman's traveling companions warned him to stay with them, but, unfortunately, Oatman did not listen. Instead, Oatman was persuaded by LeConte and decided to continue the journey with his family alone. The Oatmans left the safety of Maricopa Wells with four milk cows and two oxen to pull their wagon. According to Olive Oatman, "To Mr. Oatman this resolution brought a trial of a darker hue than any that had cast its shadows upon him as yet. He believed that starvation, or the hand of the treacherous savage, would soon bring them to an awful fate if they tarried; and with much reluctance he resolved to proceed, with no attendants or companions save his exposed and depressed family." He continued with his family alone and succumbed to what was later called the "Oatman Massacre."

The Oatman Massacre

The trek from Maricopa Wells, Arizona looked more and more dire to the Oatmans. Not only did their horse die, but the cattle which remained were so frail that the Oatman children were unable to ride them. This meant the children, whose ages ranged from 2 to 17, were required to walk the 80 miles from Maricopa Wells. They were forced to leave one of their wagons in New Mexico, because nearly all of their oxen died from exhaustion. To make matters worse, the food they brought—dried fruit, jerked meat, flour, and bacon—was nearly gone. Remember that Brewster advised them to purchase supplies for a much shorter amount of time than was needed to travel out west. Essentially, following Brewster was probably the biggest mistake Royce Oatman made for his wife and children. At this point the Oatmans had no food, no money, and no valuables to trade for supplies. To make matters worse, they still had to trudge more than 100 miles to reach an army post in California called Fort Yuma, which seemed nearly impossible in their current condition.

The Apache Indians were horribly provoked by whites who intruded on their land. The Apaches intimidated and frightened individuals along the Rio Grande. The Indians were, indeed, the greatest threat to travelers. It was only a year earlier that about 100 Apaches murdered 6 travelers in northern New Mexico. The Apaches also detained a mother, her daughter, and her servant. When the mother was finally located, she was found with an arrow through her heart. The party never found her daughter or her servant. The Oatmans had to make an exceedingly difficult decision—stay in Maricopa Wells and possibly die of famine or trek onto Fort Yuma and possibly be killed by Native Americans.

It was discussed earlier that one of the reasons Royce Oatman kept moving on with his family was because of a discussion he had with an American 19th century entomologist named John Lawrence LeConte. LeConte arrived from Fort Yuma and told the families he did not see any Indians along the trail. LeConte, who traveled with fossil and beetle specimens, was recognized as the leading authority on North American beetles and described as "the father of American beetle study". He was responsible for naming and describing nearly half of the insect "taxa" known in the United States over the course of his lifetime. LeConte seemed credible, and the Oatmans trusted his word. Numerous Native American tribes traveled and occupied the land that lay between Maricopa Wells and the Colorado River, including the dangerous Western Apaches and Yavapai. However, LeConte was adamant that he had not seen any hostile Indians along his trip. Although Oatman believed the scientist, other families did not follow Royce Oatman's lead.

The Oatmans made the decision to continue traveling on the same route. The trip across the desert was exhausting, especially for the younger children and Mary Ann. She tried to stay seated, as she was pregnant. She shaded herself from the hot sun and attempted to preserve her strength. Maybe Royce Oatman figured his wife would be safer at Camp Yuma, since she was so close to giving birth to their eighth child. Whatever the case, on February 10, 1851 the Oatmans set out on their own.

The Oatmans struck out with little food, four emaciated cows, and one wagon pulled by oxen that were famished due to lack of food. In addition, the lands they crossed were treacherous. They had to climb steep hills while carrying what few possessions remained. The Oatman family traveled all alone for eight straight days. They were abandoned six months earlier by the other families who originally planned to travel as a group from Independence, Missouri.

Seven days into their trek across the terrain, Royce Oatman came to the realization the family would not have enough supplies to make it to Fort Yuma. LeConte passed the Oatmans on his way back to Yuma. Royce wrote a letter to the fort's commander, Major S. P. Heintzelman, and asked LeConte to deliver it. Heintzelman served in the Mexican-American War and later became a major general in the Civil War, but that did not mean he had a stellar reputation. He had no desire to be at Fort Yuma; he argued with the camp surgeon, Dr. Henry

Hewit, even though his 100 men were horribly ill; and he fought with LeConte. The letter asked for horses and harnesses, stating that "there is my wife & seven children and without help sir I am confident we must perrish [sic]". This letter created controversy in the media, as a newspaper alleged failure on the part of Major Heintzelman to pursue the Indians who murdered the Oatman family.

Dr. LeConte was quoted in the California media, where he expressed his opinion that Major Heintzelman was wrong for not punishing the Indians responsible for the Oatman massacre. Major Heintzelman later wrote a letter in his defense to the San Francisco *Alta California*, which was published on July 24, 1851: "Two days *before* I received the communication from Oatman, he and his family were murdered. In the next place the robbery and murder were committed on Mexican territory and by Mexican Indians. I had not the men nor the means to send a sufficient party so far on a hostile expedition; and if I had had ten thousand men I have no authority to send an armed solider into Mexican territory to chastise Mexican Indians for any outrages they may commit, even on our citizens".

Major Heintzelman also stated he could not send a rescue party because all of his horses were being used elsewhere. It was not known if this was true or if he simply did not send anyone out because he disliked LeConte so much. Major Heintzelman blamed LeConte for the disaster: "[If] Dr. LeConte had so much charity, he should have staid [sic] and accompanied the family, particular as the woman expected daily to need his services. If he and his [companion] had staid [sic] and come on with them, they probably would not have lost their lives. Some people like charity at other people's expense". Whatever the case, Major Heintzelman was persuaded to send two soldiers and a pack of mules to see what happened to the Oatman family, but it was far too late.

Even though Major Heintzelman intensely disliked LeConte, the entomologist probably did not realize help would not be given to the Oatmans. As LeConte continued on his journey towards Fort Yuma, Oatman's letter in hand, he and his Mexican guide were confronted by a group of Indians. The Indians pretended to be friendly in order to distract them. They stole the men's horses. With no transportation, LeConte and his guide had to walk the last 100 miles to their destination. LeConte knew this would delay any rescue for Oatman and his family, so LeConte posted a warning on a nearby tree about the threat of Indians.

The Heintzelman Controversy

Did Major S. P. Heintzelman think Royce Oatman deserved the horrific massacre that took nearly his entire family and made his two daughters Indian slaves? There is a lot of controversy that surrounds how Major Heintzelman handled the entire situation. It has already been discussed that he despised the entomologist, who told Royce the Gila River area was safe from Indians. Maybe Major Heintzelman did not send a search party to find the Oatmans out of spite for LeConte, or maybe he did it out of dislike for Royce Oatman. Many other men voiced their negative opinions of Royce, and Major

Heintzelman himself was quoted as saying, "Oatman was of an obstinate & contrary disposition & would take advice from no one…he was warned of the imprudence of going it alone". What Major Heintzelman said was true; Royce Oatman was known to be overly stubborn. He was warned not to take his family away from Maricopa Falls alone, yet he pushed them on no matter the consequences. But does that mean Major Heintzelman thought Royce Oatman got what he deserved?

John R. Bartlett visited the scene of the Oatman massacre more than a year after the family was murdered. He claimed a soldier told him that Major Heintzelman, the Fort Yuma leader originally given Oatman's letter requesting help, sent a party of soldiers to recover the missing Olive and Mary Ann Oatman. However, when the soldiers arrived at the scene, they reported that they could not ascertain which Indian tribe was responsible for the atrocities committed against the Oatman family. Major Heintzelman wrote about the incident in a report from Fort Yuma on July 15, 1853 that claimed, among other things, that "In the month of February, 1851, an emigrant family was murdered on this emigrant route, about eighty miles from here. I got a letter from the man asking aid, and sent a [s]mall party to meet him; they reached the place after he was murdered".

His report went on to explain that the bodies of the Oatmans had already been buried except a son and two girls "one a child". Major Heintzelman claimed the massacre was done by the Cu-cha-nos, although it is unclear what tribe he was referencing in that allegation, as his original letter on March 27, 1851 said it was the Maricopas. He sent a letter to the San Diego headquarters stating, "I cannot believe they have been murdered & if so it is too late to pursue with any force I have the means to send". However, charges were ultimately filed against Major Heintzelman for "crew and inhuman conduct" and "neglect of duty", because he did not send out a search party right away when he learned the Oatman family was missing and could be in danger.

THE OATMANS CARRY ON

Did Royce Oatman see LeConte's warning? More than likely he did, but it was too late to turn back. Oatman had already led his family hundreds of miles across the United States. He knew they could not simply turn around and head back to Illinois, even if they wanted to. Oatman also did not know about the bad blood between Major Heintzelman and LeConte, nor did he know that his pleas for help would go unanswered. Yes, LeConte warned that there were Apaches roaming the hills, but they did not harm LeConte. As his family reached the southern bank of the Gila River on February 15th, the Indians they and other whites faced thus far changed his mind about their friendliness towards whites. Some Indians traded fairly with him, but others stole his cattle (similar to LeConte's fate with his horses). He started to remember the negative stories and experiences about the Indians. For example, when he and his group camped along the Arkansas River, a number of Apaches on the other side slaughtered a group traveling for a government excursion. Royce Oatman once gave Indians the benefit of the doubt, but now the warnings he ignored in Maricopa Wells haunted him, and he worried about the safety of his family.

The Oatmans spent the night stranded on a small island in Mexico, which was dangerously enclosed by quicksand and the Gila River, a 649-mile arm of the Colorado River that flows through New Mexico and Arizona. The family tried to cross the river's three-foot waters, but their cattle kept sinking. That was not the only danger from the river. Indigenous peoples have lived along the river for thousands of years. A group of these people were the downfall of the Oatman family.

As the family ate a small meal of bean soup and stale bread, they realized how dire their situation was. High winds endangered the warmth and shelter of the family. This caused the children to shiver throughout the night, while Lorenzo tried to manage the remaining animals the best he could. Royce Oatman broke down in tears. He knew the trouble he had led his family into, and things continued to look grim. The children saw their parents worry as they tried to go to sleep. Olive thought about what she would do if Indians attacked. She was adamant that she would not let them take her. Instead, she thought, she would rather kill herself than be taken by Indians.

Olive woke up the next morning and then, just after dawn, the Oatmans continued their trip west. They were all alone and vulnerable. By noon they were hand-carrying their things over a 200-foot bluff, since they could not travel over it by wagon. This is when Lucy revealed to her brother, Lorenzo, that she heard her father crying the night before. Their father was no longer the strong, optimistic man they had always known. He was now worried for the lives of his family. He felt something terrible was about to happen to them.

The Oatmans made their way to the top of the bluff and decided to stop for lunch before continuing on their trip under the hot sun. Then, Lorenzo saw something coming from the distance. It was a parade of Indians, and they were Yavapais. He pointed them out to his father, who looked ahead in a panic. Olive looked at the pack of Indians in the distance and counted 19 of them, while her father tried to reassure his children not to be alarmed. The last thing he said to his family was a lie: "The Indians won't harm you".

THE DEADLY YAVAPAIS

Once the family reached the banks of the Gila River, which was approximately 80 miles east of Yuma, they were ambushed by Native Americans. At first, Olive identified the Indians who murdered her family and kidnapped her and her sister as the dreaded Apaches, but it was later determined to be a group of Yavapais called the Tolkepayas. This made more sense, since this Indian tribe lived in western Arizona, which was north of the Gila and east of the Colorado Rivers. They were also rivals of the two Indian tribes who had been friendly to the Oatmans when they were in Maricopa Wells, the Pimas and the Maricopas.

On February 18th, the Oatman family was approached by a group of Yavapais (although some say they were Tonto Apache concealed as Puma Indians). The Yavapai, which

52

translates to "people of the sun," was a Native American tribe from Arizona was split into four different areas: Western, Northwestern, Southeastern, and Northeastern Yavapai.

Royce Oatman lit a pipe and shared it with the Indians, possibly hoping it would create a peaceful situation between the two groups. He also tried to speak to them in Spanish, but when he kept refusing their requests for supplies, the Indians formed a circle and started speaking in their own language. The Native Americans asked the Oatmans for tobacco and food, but Royce Oatman only shared a few resources, because his family did not have many supplies. This perceived stinginess angered the Yavapais, who demanded more from the Oatmans. Royce Oatman knew the family still had more than 80 miles to travel before they reached their destination. He knew he could not spare anything else without risking the lives of his family.

Although Royce was fearful for his family, he tried not to show it. He believed a myth that stated if you did not show fear, Indians would not attack. As brave as Royce may have appeared on the outside, hiding his fear proved to be fruitless when it came to the Indians before him. Mary Ann quickly took her three-year-old, Roland, inside the wagon for safety, while sisters Lucy and Olive stayed outside with their younger siblings. Mary Ann just sat on a rock close by. The Oatman family wanted to leave and find safety away from the Yavapais, but that did not happen.

It is unclear if Royce's decision caused the Yavapais to attack the Oatman family or if the Yavapais planned to murder the Oatmans all along. The reason for the massacre did not matter, as within minutes the Native Americans murdered Olive's parents and three children. They went after Royce first, probably to make sure the primary male of the Oatmans would not be able to protect his wife and children. Eleven-year-old Royce Jr. was killed with a single blow to the head. They pushed Olive away and went after her mother and baby sister, Charity Ann. Olive later remembered the trusting looks on her younger siblings' faces when their father reassured them that they should not fear the Indians. She also remembered the sound her father made as he convulsed and died from the attack. Royce was assaulted, and then 15-year-old Lorenzo was clubbed in the back of the dead. Lorenzo was hit so hard that he fell face down into the dirt. It took only a single blow from a club to kill Royce Jr. Then they went after Mary Ann, Roland, and Charity Ann. The Indians kidnapped 14-year-old Olive and 7-year-old Mary Ann. Only Olive and Mary Ann were spared. They did not know the blow to the head did not kill their older brother.

Lorenzo regained consciousness and heard the repeated yells and shrieks of the Natives as a counterpoint to his dying family's cries: "Help, help! In the name of God, cannot any one help us?". The Yavapais even dragged the boy by his feet and threw him off the edge of the mesa along with his dying mother, who cried while she and her unborn baby died. Although Lorenzo was left for dead, he miraculously survived the brutal attack and went in search of his sisters. At first, Lorenzo thought it was just a matter of time until he, too, succumbed to his injuries. His scalp had been torn during the attack, and blood still oozed from his nose and ears, yet he was able to get up and move to safety. He looked around until the unspeakable memory of what happened flew back into his mind.

Lorenzo moved his battered body up a hill and crawled the 50 feet he was thrown by the Yavapais. When he got to the top of the incline, he saw his family's dead bodies lying in the dirt. He hurried back towards Maricopa Falls, hoping the Indians did not see him. Lorenzo walked 15 miles until he was overcome with dehydration and starvation. He passed out for a few hours before he was awakened by a pack of gray wolves. He yelled and batted at one, threw a stone at another, and scared them away. As Lorenzo moved forward, he noticed the pack trailing him ever so slightly. Luckily, the wolves stopped, huddled together, and then wandered away from Lorenzo. He was safe again, for now.

Lorenzo was ravenous, with only scraps of bread he found by his family's dead bodies to sustain him. He knew deep down those scraps would not carry him on to Maricopa Falls. He considered eating the flesh from his arm at one point. As Lorenzo traveled on, he came across the one thing he feared most—Indians. Luckily, this time the Indians were the Pimas. One remembered Lorenzo as the oldest Oatman boy. According to Lorenzo himself, "he embraced me with every expression of pity and condolence that would throb in an American heart" ("Apache captives' ordeal," 2021, para. 16). The two Pima Indians gave Lorenzo bread and water as well as a blanket to lay on while they left to investigate the massacre. They returned with some of his dead family's possessions. They personally guided Lorenzo back to Maricopa Wells. Lorenzo had been saved, and he had been saved by Indians.

As the small party traveled, Lorenzo saw in the distance wagons that belonged to two families from his original group. One of the men, Robert Kelly, took one look at Lorenzo's battered, bloodstained body and asked, "My God, Lorenzo, what in the name of heaven has happened?". Lorenzo told them that the Oatman family was slaughtered by Indians. He and his former traveling companions cried. Lorenzo made it safely back to the rest of the group, and then some of the men rode back out to where the Oatman family was massacred. The flesh on the dead bodies of their Mormon friends had been eaten by coyotes, and there was no way to bury Royce, Mary Ann, and their children in the hardened ground.

It is nearly impossible to believe that, although Lorenzo awoke to find his parents and four siblings dead, in addition to sustaining severe injuries himself, he maintained enough strength to struggle through the dangerous and risky Arizona landscape for help. Yet he ultimately reached a settlement where his injuries were treated, and he eventually returned to his original group of Mormons. When Lorenzo was strong enough to return to the place where the bodies of his family remained, he was quoted as stating "We buried the bodies of father, mother and babe in one common grave". First, Lorenzo dealt with the bodies of his family. They could not dig graves in the volcanic rocky soil, so they instead collected the bodies together and formed a man-made pile of stones over them for a gravesite. Then, he became determined to keep searching for his two living siblings, Olive and Mary Ann. Once Lorenzo was finally well, he and his party were ready to continue on to California. With the help and protection of seven army deserters, Lorenzo and the other Mormon men laid in the bed of the wagons and headed out.

The weird thing about this entire tragic situation was that the Yavapais usually stayed clear of people who traveled along the Gila Trail. The Oatman massacre and the kidnapping of Olive and Mary Ann did not make a lot of sense. The violence against the Oatmans was more than likely due to the destitution the Yavapais faced throughout the winter months. They may have been desperate at this point, which is perhaps why they stole LeConte's horses only a few days before asking Royce Oatman for food. When he refused to share his supplies, they killed his family and his cows, then ate the animal meat. But why did they kidnap Olive and Mary Ann instead of killing them with the rest of the family? Why abduct two white girls who would end up just being two more mouths to feed?

Were the abductions revenge against whites, or were the girls to be traded for ransom at a later date? Would they be used as food, since the Yavapais were desperate for nourishment? It is true that in the past the Yavapais performed cannibalism. They roasted a girl alive and ate her after they were attacked by the Halchidhoma Indians. The story was that much more disturbing, as it was rumored the poor girl's mother was forced to eat some of her. Would Olive and Mary Ann succumb to the same horrible fate? This was going through Olive's mind, but the answer was no. Olive and Mary Ann were captured for one reason and one reason only—the Yavapais meant to enslave them. More specifically, they would be slaves to the Yavapais' women and children. The women were in charge of harvesting the tribe's crops with the children as well as preparing the food. Slaves to help with these laborious duties were probably welcomed.

The two Oatman girls watched in shock as the Indians first killed their family, then looted their wagon. One group of the Indians took the family's cows and oxen, while the other group took the two captives and headed out of Mexico back into the United States. The girls were, indeed, made slaves of the Yavapai. They traveled with the natives for hours, falling over rocks because they were weak from lack of food. The only food the girls were offered was the paltry amount left from their family's own wagon. According to Olive herself, "We thought they would kill us and hoped they would do so". But they did not kill the girls. They made them walk barefoot so the imprints of their shoes would not be recognized by others, and it would be harder for them to escape. They traveled 60 miles over 4 days.

At first, Olive thought the women were slaves to the men, since they walked behind the men, but that was far from the case. There was a division of labor among the Yavapais, and the women for the most part were not subservient to the men. During their time living among the Yavapais, Olive and Mary Ann spent their days doing laborious chores, from digging roots, to carrying water in pots, to collecting wood from miles around the Indian camp. As Olive explained of this awful time in her life, the sisters became slaves to the enslaved. That is, the women were the workers and enjoyed whipping Olive and Mary Ann when they did not fulfill their requests. Olive explained further that, "Their women were the laborers and principal burden-bearers, and during all our captivity...it was our lot to serve under these enslaved women, with a severity more intolerable than that to which they were subjected by their merciless lords".

This began the tale that has lived on for generations in books, plays, poetry, films, and television shows. Olive Oatman and her sister, Mary Ann, spent a year as slaves to the Yavapai Indians before being traded to the Mohaves. The Mohaves raised the girls as their own and them with tattoos. Mary Ann did not survive the years of captivity, but Olive did. She eventually returned to her white counterparts. However, the tattoo on her chin forever remained a symbol of her time as a pioneer girl turned Native American.

CAPTOR 1 – THE YAVAPAIS TRIBE

When Olive and Mary Ann Oatman were made captives of the Yavapais Tribe, they slowly adjusted to their new lives as slaves. The Indians traveled in two groups over the course of harsh days and nights. One group led Olive and Mary Ann, while the other group led the animals. The Yavapais made camp overnight and killed one of the cows for food. The men cooked the dead animal over a fire and used the Oatman family's own flour to bake dough soaked in bean soup. They mockingly offered some of the food to the sisters, making fun of the fact that their father claimed he did not have enough food to spare. Although the Indians offered Olive and Mary Ann boiled beans and little cakes made from flour, the girls refused. The sisters did not eat a thing. They could not even bear to try. Instead, they just watched their captors in silence and ignored their hunger.

Horrible thoughts ran through Olive's head. Would she and her younger sister be burned alive? Would they be eaten by the natives? These thoughts, and the thoughts about the family that was now gone, terrified the two young girls, who had lost everything. Throughout the night the Indians heckled the girls as they hunched together, frightened and uncertain of their future. Olive herself explained the feelings she had for her sister and how Mary Ann would "hide her head in my arms, and most piteously sob aloud".

In 1851 news of the Oatmans' demise reached the whites living in California. The story of a family who traveled via the old Santa Fe route met by dangerous natives about 70 miles from Fort Yuma spread across the west. It was a disastrous and unimaginable true tale of a family with a lack of supplies, dangerous terrain, and exhaustion who met a horrible fate at the hands of Apache savages. The story disseminated reported that seven family members were murdered and two of the Oatman girls were kidnapped. They also knew that Lorenzo Oatman, clubbed and left for dead, narrowly escaped with serious wounds. However, no one had heard a peep from either Olive or Mary Ann.

In one moment Olive Oatman's life changed forever. She yearned to go back and take one last look at her parents and siblings who lost their lives during the massacre. The Yavapais taunted her by occasionally pointing to the Oatmans' wagon, which lay bare and was the only visible reminder of her family.

Traveling barefoot to their new home with the Yavapais was treacherous. The Yavapais made the girls walk for hours so they were not discovered by whites near the site of the Oatman massacre. After several hours the sisters, whose feet bled, were exhausted and in pain. However, if they tried to slow down, the Yavapais threatened them with their clubs. Mary Ann's legs could not take any more, and at one point she collapsed. The Yavapais beat her and threatened to leave her behind if she did not get up. Despondent, she pleaded with her sister to let the Yavapais kill her.

Olive begged them to spare her younger sister's life and not leave her behind. One of the Indians showed a bit of mercy. He took off his backpack, handed it to another man, and took Mary Ann onto his back. Olive tried to speak to her sister, but Mary Ann did not answer. Exhausted and weakened, the younger Oatman sister simply collapsed on the Indian's body as they continued their journey towards the tribe's home. At one point as the group hiked on for more than a day, Mary Ann went into shock.

The Yavapais refused to take more than one short break throughout the night and into the afternoon of the next day. When the group finally took a two-hour break to make dinner and rest, the girls ate the first meal with their captors. The Yavapais killed the rest of the animals they took from Olive and Mary Ann's parents and made a meal of meat, bread, and bean soup. Mary Ann gave up at this point. The Indians demanded she walk and, when she refused, they beat her again, then carried her on their backs. Olive's bloody feet were wrapped in leather so she could hike to another rest stop. When they arrived, the girls simply fell asleep in the sand.

The girls woke up the next day, had another meal, then hiked for a long time. Her will to live, even if it was only to protect her younger sister, began to wane. Hiking became unbearable, and Olive pleaded with her captors to kill her. They did not; instead, the Yavapais continued the painful trip to their home.

If things were not bad enough for Olive and Mary Ann Oatman, the Yavapais met about a dozen Comanches during their trip. The Comanches had a reputation for fierceness during battle as well as revolting and repulsive methods of torture. The tales about the Comanche tribe included butchering babies, roasting their enemies alive, gang-raping white women, and riding thousands of miles just to wipe out one family. One of the most infamous tales of torture was that of a young girl around Olive's age named Matilda Lockhart, who was abducted by the Comanche Indians in 1838. When she was finally returned to her family two years later, she was unrecognizable. Her body was covered in burns and bruises, and her nose was burned off her face. According to writer Mary Ann Maverick, who witnessed Matilda's return, she "was utterly degraded, and could not hold up her head again. Her head, arms, and face were full of bruises, and sores, and her nose actually burnt off to the bone-all the fleshy end gone, and a great scab formed e on the end of the bone. Both nostrils were wide open and denuded of flesh. She told a piteous tale of how dreadfully the Indians had beaten her, and how they would wake her from her sleep by sticking a chunk of fire to her flesh, especially to her nose...her body had many scars from the fire".

It was said that Matilda's six-year-old sister was one of the girls who was pegged outside naked, skinned, sliced, horribly mutilated, and then burned alive by Comanche women. If Olive and Mary Ann Oatman knew any of these stories, they more than likely feared their time had nearly come to a similar horrible end.

One of the Comanche Indians who spotted Olive immediately shot an arrow at her, which, luckily, only pierced her dress. Olive later found out that same Indian lost his brother to white men and vowed to kill the next white person he saw. The Yavapais and the Comanche nearly fought. One group of the Yavapais stayed to argue with the violent Comanches, while the other group of Yavapais rushed Olive and Mary Ann away from the scene. What Mary Ann disclosed to Olive next was very telling of how dire their situation was: "I wish they had killed us".

The trek to their new home as slaves took only four days, but it probably seemed like the longest four days of the Oatman girls' lives. Olive and Mary Ann reached a part of Arizona surrounded by hills in an area today known as Congress. Present day Congress, Arizona is located in Yavapai County. Yes, the county is named after Olive and Mary Ann's captors. Today the county has two Indian communities, the Yavapai-Apache Nation and the Yavapai-Prescott Tribe. As noted by the current name of the county, it acknowledged the Yavapais and their influence on this region.

The first part of the Oatman girls' lives in captivity was spent with the Western Yavapai tribe called the Tolkepayas. Olive later identified her first captors as the Tonto Apache tribe, which was one of the groups of Western Apache people. However, it is likely that the Indians who bludgeoned her family to death, stole their belongings, and captured Olive and her sister were belonged to the Yavapais tribe of the Tolkepayas.

After several days of treacherous travel, Olive and her sister saw a village on the horizon. The Tolkepayas tribe lived eight miles southwest of Aguila, Arizona in the highest mountain range of southwestern Arizona called the Harquahala Mountains. Olive described it as "a cluster of low, thatched huts, each having an opening near the ground." As they arrived in this unknown village, Olive thought she and her sister would soon be killed. They were not. Instead, Olive and Mary Ann spent the next year as slaves to the Tolkepayas.

The humiliation as slaves began right away, when 300 Yavapai citizens—men, women, and children—surrounded their new prisoners for inspection. Olive and Mary Ann were forced to stand on a heap of branches and twigs in the center of the large group of Yavapai. They were on display while the Yavapai, donned in blankets, animal skins, or nothing at all, peered at them with a curious scrutiny. As music played, the humiliation continued when the Yavapai threw dirt at the girls, spat on them, and yelled at them. Olive's take on this behavior was that "their main ambition was to exhibit their superiority over us". The girls were terrified of their fate. Would they experience the same rape and disfigurement as Matilda Lockhart, or would they be tortured to death? No, the Yavapai did not intend to torture the two white girls; they intended to make them slaves.

The Yavapais were mountain occupants. The men hunted deer, rabbit, sheep, and quail; guarded the camp; built the huts; and dressed the skins. They ate meat as well as various plants and roots, but the Yavapais did not allow women to eat meat unless they were nearly dead. Because of this practice, the young female children often did not live to be adults. The female Yavapais who did survive were usually sickly and dwarfish, according to Olive. Women were also strictly forbidden from eating meat while they were menstruating and after giving birth. They planted corn, squash, and beans along the banks of rivers and streams with the hope of floods to water the plants. If food was limited, the Yavapais ate caterpillars and grasshoppers, something that disgusted Olive. But it was better than nothing, as Olive remembered entire days without a crumb. When a hunter returned with game and he was surrounded by hungry Yavapais, he simply threw scraps at Olive and explained how, in the minds of the Yavapais, the girls were fed too well. Their captors actually thought they treated Olive and Mary Ann better than they should, and they had to teach them to live on as little as possible. The girls watched as the Yavapais satisfied their own insatiable appetites. Only then would the girls possibly be given a morsel of food, with the hope that maybe the dogs, who were probably treated better, would share some of their leftovers.

The men used clay pots to boil meat, something both Olive and Mary Ann saw firsthand on their long travels to the Yavapais camp. It was strange that the Oatman girls were offered meat at all while making the trek to the Yavapais camp, since the girls were given barely anything once they arrived. Probably one of the most shocking differences between the white girls and the Yavapais were their clothes, or lack thereof. Olive was made to dress like the Yavapais women, including a two-piece belted buckskin outfit with a strap around her neck. Unmarried Yavapais women sometimes rolled tin into the hems of their skirts. The Yavapais men simply wore a buckskin shirt tied in front with fringes on their shoulders. The Yavapais children were naked until the ages of 9 or10.

The women cared about their appearance and had peculiar rituals for beauty. For example, they were told not to smile when they were menstruating, because that would cause wrinkles. They were also told to break branches off trees when gathering wood, because it would make their breasts grow. They were advised not to bend over to gather wood, because it would make their breasts sag. The Yavapais decorated their faces, and by their mid-teens most males had face tattoos. Women also had tattoos on their chins so their relatives could greet them after they died. Olive's tattoo made her famous years later when she left the Yavapais and lived with another tribe. But as slaves of the Yavapais, the girls were not submitted to the pain of tattoos, because the Yavapais did not care about Olive and Mary Ann's souls after they died.

The girls assimilated the best they could by learning the Yavapai language so they could at least understand the orders given to them. Mary Ann was not as strong as Olive and had a much harder time as a slave. Sickly when she lived a normal life with her family in La Harpe, the rigors of slave life, which required day after day of heavy labor with little food, took its toll on Mary Ann's health. When she got sick, the Yavapais did not care and still expected her to complete her slave tasks each day. If she did not complete her work, she was beaten, which made matters worse.

The year with the Tolkepaya tribe of the Yavapais was not kind to Olive and Mary Ann. Things got so bad for Olive and Mary Ann that they planned an escape from their captivity. However, they were too scared to go through with it. In their minds, they would live the rest of their sad lives as slaves to the Yavapais. Over the course of their year with the tribe, they were forced to scavenge for food as well as haul water and firewood. They were whipped if they dropped anything, then ridiculed, scorned, and beaten. The Yavapais had a high respect for stamina and endurance. If the girls could not keep up, this was a sign of weakness. If the girls complained while being beaten for not completing their laborious tasks, this was also seen as a sign of weakness and, in the mind of the Yavapais, deserved more torture. In addition, the food the Yavapais procured was never for them; if they did not fend for themselves, they would ultimately starve. The Oatman girls did not know that a visit from a group of Mohave Indians would change their lives forever.

In 1851 the United States boundary commissioner, John Russell Bartlett, traveled through California and Arizona to commemorate the new border between the United States and Mexico. An American historian and linguist, Bartlett was the commissioner from 1850 through 1853 and held the responsibility of surveying this boundary between the two countries. During the summer of 1851 he spent weeks with the Pimas and the Maricopas and inquired about the Oatman massacre. The friendly Indians told Bartlett what they knew about the murders and the kidnappings of Olive and Mary Ann, but they did not know where the sisters were taken. Bartlett told them he would reward anyone who found Olive and Mary Ann Oatman and returned them to Fort Yuma.

Meanwhile, Olive and Mary Ann started to learn a thing or two about how to handle themselves with the Yavapais. They established a daily routine as slaves and learned how to build up their endurance, since the Yavapais held it in such high regard. During the day they simply obeyed the demands of the women and children; then at night they tried to slip away together to pray. They spent some of their nights sitting around the campfire listening to the Yavapai men tell stories of their youth. At this point, the Yavapais started to relax a little with Olive and Mary Ann, as the girls were more fluent speaking the Yavapais language.

Since Olive and Mary Ann were able to communicate with the Yavapais, they sat and had conversations together. The Yavapais were shocked to learn how far the Oatman family traveled from their home in Illinois. The women in particular asked the sisters various questions, such as how many white people were there, did they own the world east of the Atlantic, or how far did the ocean go. They also wondered about the relationships between men and women, such as how the women were treated and whether or not American men had multiple wives. This was not because the Yavapais practiced polygamy. It was quite the opposite. If a Yavapais man caught his wife with another man, there was a chance the lover would not survive the night, or the wife of the adulterer would either fight the mistress or simply take her children away from her. No, the Yavapais were monogamous; the Yavapais women were simply curious as to how the white Americans lived. Olive and Mary Ann were essentially their first connection with this outside world.

As the Yavapais and the sisters communicated on a level beyond the relationship of slave and owner, they became more merciful to the girls, especially toward the frail and sickly Mary Ann. The women who had control over Mary Ann's daily labors were kinder to her, taken by her patient and enduring spirit. They had a belief that the world had been destroyed and reborn three separate times. The most recent time the world was destroyed, in their opinion, was in the red rock area of Sedona, and a fourth apocalypse was forthcoming. The girls discussed their Mormon religion with the Indians, explaining how "of the well-founded belief they had that the stars above us were peopled by human beings, and of the fact that the distance to these far-off worlds had been measured by the whites". The tribe was skeptical of these white Mormon beliefs, especially their take on the stars above. The women claimed that if there were, indeed, people within the stars, they would certainly drop out of them. Since they had obviously not seen anyone dropping out of the sky, they knew this belief was a lie. They asked Olive sarcastically if they had ever been there. Had they seen these stars that were populated by individuals? The Yavapais believed that an evil spirit ruled the whites, and this evil spirit was guiding them towards destruction. Although the Yavapais probably did not believe Olive's stories of people and stars, the conversations had a positive effect on her captors. The girls became humans to them, not just slaves. The Yavapais found their conversations entertaining, to say the least. So, their treatment towards Olive and Mary Ann improved.

Captor 2 – The Mohaves

In the autumn of 1851, after a year of torture and torment living with the Yavapais, a group of Mohave Native Americans visited the Tolkepayas camp to trade. The Mohaves were friendly with the Yavapais and other tribes like the Quechans. They were enemies of the Pimas, the Maricopas, and the Cocopas and merely tolerated the Chemchuevis. The Mohaves visited the Yavapais for their annual trading run and brought vegetables to trade for furs. Olive was immediately impressed by the Mohaves, as they seemed superior to the Yavapais in many ways. First and foremost, the Mohaves seemed much more intelligent than the Yavapais. Olive observed that just by the way they carried themselves and communicated with their counterparts.

The daughter of Mohave Chief Espaniole, Topeka, saw how the Oatman girls were treated by the Tolkepayas. Olive described Topeka as beautiful and sympathetic toward the girls. Topeka saw how unhappy the two white girls were living with the Yavapais and bargained for their release. At first, she tried to make a trade for the sisters, but the Yavapais refused. When no agreement was reached, Topeka and the Mohaves left without Olive and Mary Ann. However, Topeka did not give up. She was tenacious and returned to again offer a trade for the sisters.

The Yavapais spent hours discussing the positives and negatives of trading Olive and Mary Ann to the Mohaves. Their utmost concern was revenge from the United States government. Would they retaliate against the Yavapais for brutally killing the Oatman family and kidnapping two young white girls? This retaliation could be deadly for the Yavapais tribe. On the other hand, trading them to the Mohaves would give the Yavapais much needed supplies. It was late in 1851, just a year after a drought that severely limited their food. Trading the sisters could also stave off any trouble with the whites, since the Mohaves were a more remote tribe. Mary Ann overheard these discussions and told her sister.

Olive related to Mary Ann her positive impressions of the Mohaves when they first arrived and how the girls' lives might improve by living with them. However, what if the Mohaves were just trying to make a good impression? What if they treated the sisters worse than the Yavapais? The girls soon realized that nothing was worse than the Yavapais; even death was preferable to staying with the Yavapais. Mary Ann in particular got weaker by the day. The girls survived only on roots, and Olive was aware of Mary Ann's gaunt look. Her cheeks were pale, and her eyes were sunken. Mary Ann was sick with a cold and dreaded another long journey to a new camp. She feared she would never survive an experience like that again.

Olive and Mary Ann Oatman continued living with the Yavapais until the spring of 1852 when Topeka and five Mohave men returned to the Yavapais village. Chief Espaniole sent his 17-year-old daughter back to the Yavapais to make a deal with the Oatman girls' captors. Topeka was definitely persuasive. Not only did she speak the Yavapais language, but she carried herself with a mixture of sweetness and intelligence. However, the Yavapais still were not convinced and discussed it throughout the night, while Olive and Mary Ann waited patiently in their hut. The tribe members who killed the Oatman family objected to trading Olive and Mary Ann due to fear of retaliation for their heinous crimes. Other Yavapais who spent some time with the sisters asked them directly if they wanted to go with the Mohaves. For example, one Yavapai woman who spent so much time with the girls that she learned some English told Olive and Mary Ann her worries. She said the Mohaves would either sell them to someone else or simply kill them. She told Olive and Mary Ann that she wanted them to be free, but she did not think the Mohave tribe would ever return them to the whites. The Mohaves, on the other hand, explained that they wanted to trade for Olive and Mary Ann out of kindness, plain and simple. Topeka in particular wanted to save the girls from cruel treatment at the hands of the Yavapais. Finally, the Yavapais gave in and by sunset traded

Olive and Mary Ann for two horses, vegetables, three blankets, and beads.

The Yavapais gave Olive and Mary Ann the goodbye and send-off they expected, laughter and insults. However, a few of the Yavapai children cried because their white caregivers were leaving them. Olive and Mary Ann were each given a pound of beef, which, along with any roots they found along the way, was their only food for the next 10 days. The sisters were finally free of the Yavapais, but again had a long journey ahead of them.

Mary Ann's fears of another treacherous trip to a new camp were soon reinforced. The Mohaves traveled so quickly that within a day Olive and Mary Ann's feet were raw. However, the way the Mohaves reacted was much different from the Yavapais. Instead of insults and beatings for not keeping up, the Mohaves made them provisional shoes from skins and told the girls they would travel shorter distances each day. At night Topeka gave the sisters blankets to sleep in the sand.

After 11 days of travel Olive and Mary Ann Oatman reached their next home, the Mohave Valley. It was a beautiful green region that spread through mountains. The Mohaves lived on both sides of the Colorado River, the border of California, and the future Arizona. Mary Ann was impressed and said what was probably the first positive thing since her capture: "Isn't it a beautiful valley?...It seems to me I should live here". Today this area is in Needles, California. Ironically, they finally reached the promised land Charles Brewster called "Bashan."

The Oatman sisters were immediately taken to the family of a tribal leader, Espaniole (his non-Mohave name), who lived in a 100-foot clearing of trees above the water. Espaniole was a festival chief, which meant he planned dances for the tribe and managed the celebrations. For example, when the Mohaves had a good harvest, they celebrated with a grand feast. When Olive attended her first celebration with the tribe, she could not believe the social gathering compared to her time with the serious and somber Yavapais. The Mohaves either painted their faces or wore bark masks and danced by a fire well past midnight.

The next day they feasted on cakes, boiled vegetables, and soups, then danced for another 12 hours. She commented on the overt sexual practices of the Mohaves that made a Mormon girl blush: "On this occasion I witnessed some of the most shameful indecencies, on the part of both male and female, that came to my eye for the five years of my stay among Indians". She learned that the Mohaves viewed sex as fun and natural, which was not what the Mormon religion taught. Many of the Mohave children saw their parents or others having sex at a very young age, and young girls were encouraged to have sex soon after they started menstruating. They also did not assign one's gender at birth; instead, they accepted transvestism and did not consider one's gender to be permanent until after puberty. The Mohaves were truly ahead of their time.

Other celebratory events that Olive and Mary Ann probably had to get used to were victory parties after battle. The Mohaves engaged in scalp-dancing, which included both socializing and, of course, sex. The men and women painted themselves like warriors, showed the trophy scalps won during battle, and then sought partners. These celebrations often motivated new marriages among the Mohave men and women.

Espaniole planned fun events but also was responsible for captives. This may have been why his daughter was so taken with Olive and Mary Ann right away. If her father was in charge of captives, then she probably also saw how he treated them versus the treatment given by the Yavapais. Although serious, Olive viewed Espaniole as a mild-mannered man who promoted a sense of unity within the tribe. In his opinion, everyone should help one another. As such, this family treated the girls much differently than their former captors. They treated the girls not like slaves, but like family. Olive later expressed her profound love and affection for her new Mohave family, particularly her new "mother" and "sister." The tribal leader, his wife, Aespaneo, and their daughter, Topeka, took an immediate interest in the girls' well-being. The girls noticed that the Mohave tribe was much more prosperous than their former captors. Aespaneo and Topeka offered Olive and Mary Ann blankets when they were cold. The family also gifted plots of land, and the sisters grew some of their own food.

Right away Olive noticed how loving and caring Aespaneo was to her children. She acted like her daughter, Topeka, had been gone for months, not merely a few weeks. Although she could not speak to Olive due to the language barrier, Aespaneo gave her a warm smile. Topeka quickly grabbed a cake she saw roasting and tore it into pieces for the girls. Again, this was much different from the roots that were thrown at the girls by the Yavapais to eat, then told they were given too much. When Olive and Mary Ann were first brought to the village of the Yavapais, they were taunted, and things were thrown at them. In contrast, the Mohaves celebrated the girls' appearance with dancing and singing.

Although the history of the Mohaves was not recorded in writing, it appears they inhabited the Mohave Valley near the Colorado River in the Mojave Desert for 1,000 years or more, and during that time avoided the outside influence of others. Whether Mexicans, Spaniards, or Americans, the Mohaves lived in peace with their neighbors. For example, in 1776 Father Francisco Hermenegildo Garcés of Spain was guided by the Mohaves when he visited the area of the Colorado River. Garcés was a Spanish Franciscan friar from Tucson, an outpost of New Spain, who served as both a missionary and an explorer of southwestern North America. Garcés was the first non-Indian to cross the Mojave Desert route and go into Alta California. He was also the first individual to discover the Mojave River and the first to attempt to open a road from Mission San Luis Obispo, a Spanish mission founded in 1772 by Father Junípero Serra in Alta California, to the capital of New Mexico at Santa Fe called the Villa Real. His first mission on his own began in January 1776 when he made friends with the Mohaves and referred to them as "Jamajab."

The Mohaves provided a few of their young men to serve as Garcés' guides through the desert and Pacific Coast. He estimated that the population of the Mohaves was 3,000, although they were probably closer to 4,000. Garcés carried a banner that showed the Virgin Mary, for whom the Mohaves felt affection, on one side and a sinner burning in hell on the other side. According to Garcés' diary on March 4th: "1 departed [from the river] on a course southwest, and in two leagues and a half arrived at some wells which I named Pozos de San Casimiro. The Mohaves guided Garcés southwest from the river instead of going northwest towards the Piute Spring. Garcés described the Mohaves as having a "gentle and sincere character". Garcés established two mission churches along the lower Colorado River and the Yuma Crossing, the home of the Quechans discussed earlier. Spanish settlers maintained a peaceful relationship with the Quechans, and Garcés tried to maintain this peace between the Spaniards and Native Americans. Unfortunately, Garcés was killed during an uprising of Quechans enraged over Spanish soldiers who followed Garcés and took over their land.

The Mohaves were not always gentle and sincere. When fur trappers Jedediah Smith and Kit Carson appeared on the Mohave land in the 1820s, they caused more than a decade of violence between the whites and the Mohaves. Smith was a legendary trapper and explorer who, unfortunately, had bouts of violence with the Native Americans. His ribs were shattered and his scalp partially torn off during a mauling by a bear. In 1830 he was attacked and killed by Comanche Indians as he traveled along the Santa Fe Trail. Carson was also a well-known frontiersman who led a series of campaigns to try to pacify the Navajo and other Southwestern Indian tribes such as the Mohaves. Their fights with Smith, Carson, and others built a reputation of being brutal warriors, but their actions were often instigated by leaders who initiated hostilities among the Mohaves. The Mohaves didn't start the fight; instead, they were usually sucked into battle to protect their territory, to exact revenge, or to enhance their identity in a nationalistic or spiritual way. Their warriors were born, not trained, and they pulled authority and power from childhood dreams. Dreams were an inspiration for war and a foundation for the Mohave consciousness. That meant you were not born into status; instead, your dreams propelled you into warfare. In addition, they approached war like a sport, where scalps and captives were their trophies. The Mohave women danced around these scalps while they also cried for the warriors they lost.

However, there were explorers who saw the good in the Mohaves, especially when compared to their Yavapai counterparts. For example, Baldwin Mollhausen during his journey to the Pacific documented in a diary that the Yavapai were "small hideous figures of the first and the cunning repulsive expression of their faces" and the Mohaves as "finely-developed forms, as they came bounding towards us in immense leaps over stones and bushes, with the agility of black-tailed deer, and their pleasant, almost open looks, which even their frightful style of decoration could not disguise". Mollhausen also commented on the Mohaves' good humor, playfulness, laughter, and joking, something Olive and Mary Ann probably never saw with the Yavapais. This portion of his diary was printed in volume 31 of *The Spectator*. White pioneers documented the horrid actions of the Yavapais versus the pleasurable and welcoming ones of the Mohaves. Olive also viewed them in a light similar to Mollhausen's account. She did not see the Mohaves as brutal warriors but as a gentle, caring, and familial tribe.

Even after the warm welcome, Olive and Mary Ann were slow to trust the Mohaves after the year spent with the Yavapais. The Mohaves took prisoners in the past and used them as workers or symbols of a war victory. These prisoners included women who were handed over as companions to the older Mohave men, and children who were adopted into a Mohave family. Now, these captives were usually not abused or neglected as Olive and Mary Ann were by the Yavapais, but they were captives nonetheless. So, what was in it for the Mohaves to trade for Olive and Mary Ann? The sisters were not a symbol of a victory against whites or the Yavapais. Would they be married off to an older Mohave man or used as a pawn in negotiations with whites? Was the trade for the sisters really out of kindness, as the Mohaves alleged?

Yes, it seemed that kindness was the motivator, since Olive and Mary Ann were treated like family right away. It was later discovered that the tribal leader, Espaniole, had an ulterior motive trading for the girls, but it was not negative or malicious. He simply hoped that the Mohave's positive treatment of Olive and Mary Ann Oatman would encourage the whites to give the Mohaves positive treatment in return. However, the sisters still lived with Native Americans, not family or friends from their Anglo Mormon past. As Olive noted, she and her sister were "plunged now into the depths of a wild country, where the traces of a white foot would be sought in vain for hundreds of miles, and at such a distance from the nearest route of the hurrying emigrant, as to preclude almost the traveling of hope to their exile and gloom". In other words, the Oatman sisters were now deeper into seclusion with no chance of whites finding them. Olive did not know that she and Mary Ann were on the border of California, the coveted Bashan, closer to their father's original goal of Fort Yuma than when they lived with the Yavapais.

Life with the Mohaves was a welcome change from the Yavapais. The girls mastered the Mohave language quickly and engaged in energetic and animated conversations with their hosts. Olive and Mary Ann were also happy to help the Mohave girls and women with their daily chores, even though they were similar to what they were forced to do for the Yavapais. Both tribes had the girls carry water and wood, but it was different when done as a family member, not as a slave who was beaten at every turn.

However, her criticism of their farming methods was noted in Stratton's book, *Captivity of the Oatman Girls Among the Apache and Mohave Indians*. The Mohaves farmed along the Colorado River, but Olive explained that they only planted enough to last four months. She could not comprehend why they spent so much time and effort for such a small return.

According to Olive herself, "the Colorado had overflown during the winter, and there had been considerable rain. The Mohaves were in high hopes for a bountiful crop during this season. What was to them a rich harvest would be considered in Yankee land, or in the Western states, a poor compensation for so much time and plodding labor". Olive criticized a young Mohave man named Cccarekae for what she considered lazy farming habits which produced such poor results. He responded by telling her, "We have enough to satisfy us; you Americanos (a term they learned from the Mexicans) work hard, and it does you no good; we enjoy ourselves". How did Olive respond? She simply told him, "Well, we enjoy ourselves well at home, and all our white people seem happier than any Indian I have seen since".

When the sisters were not farming, they were playing games, running races, or swimming naked in the Colorado River with the Mohave girls. It was a fun and accepting time compared to life with the Yavapais. The Mohaves embraced the Oatmans' religion and paid them with beads and flannel to help ensure the girls sang their Sunday school hymns. Olive explained that the Mormons worshipped a god in the sky, but the Mohaves did not worship a god or have religious ceremonies. Instead, they focused on spiritual guidance from their primary spirit called Matavilya, the son of Earth and Sky. Matavilya gave the Mohaves their names and their commandments. They believe he is buried on the top of Spirit Mountain on the west bank of the Colorado River. According to the Mohave's faith, Matavilya killed a sea monster called Sky Rattlesnake before flying away. This was the center of their faith and determined how they viewed the afterlife. In addition, the Mohave women wore markings on their chins which allowed them access to their relatives after death.

THE INFAMOUS MARKINGS

Olive assimilated into her new Mohave culture. She learned the Mohave language and dressed according to their customs. A permanent reminder of her time with the Mohaves was prominently displayed on her face. It is said that the tribal leader, Espaniole, brought two doctors to the Oatman girls and told them since they now belonged to the Mohave tribe they should be tattooed. What happened next is not clear, but presumably Olive and Mary Ann went out with the men and laid in the grass, where charcoal designs were tattooed on their chins.

In Stratton's book, *Captivity of the Oatman Girls Among the Apache and Mohave Indians,* Olive explained the markings in a negative tone. She described this meeting with Espaniole as something she was against, saying "they would not put those ugly marks upon our faces". She also explained how the Mohaves said they knew she objected to tattoos, because she expected to leave them one day and return to the whites, but the Indians wanted Olive and Mary Ann to remain with them. She further said the Mohaves explained that if they escaped and were found by another Indian tribe, the markings meant that Olive and Mary Ann knew the Mohaves. However, Olive explained that she knew the tattoos would mark her as an

"Indian savage" if she ever returned to her "white world." She thought it would reduce her chances of living a normal life if she left the Mohaves. She would be considered an outsider, a foreigner, maybe even a freak. Little did she know that her facial markings would make her a household name, and she would still find love when she returned to the whites.

The Oatman girls were decorated with permanent tattooed markings on their chins and arms. This process was relatively simple. A shaman pricked the skin to form decorative lines. Olive described the process: "They then pricked the skin in small regular rows on our chins with a very sharp stick, until they bled freely. They then dipped these same sticks in the juice of a certain weed that grew on the banks of the river, and then in the powerful of a blue stone that was to be found in low water". Olive said the process took a few hours and was a bit painful but not as painful as the recovery.

The sisters' tattoos were more than likely made using cactus spine, as they left deep, embedded lines into their skin. Whether they were used to identify the girls as Mohave or simply for decoration, they removed them further from their old worlds. Since both tattoos were made in straight, clean lines, the girls probably did not struggle. Although Mary Ann's tattoo patterns were not recorded before her untimely death, Olive had five thick vertical bars which stretched across her jaw line and lower lip, as well as two horizontal cones on each side. Olive was the first known tattooed white woman in the United States. In addition to the tattoos on her face, Olive also sported a vertical band tattoo on her upper arms common for Mohave women.

Tattoos for women are commonplace today, but in the 1800s it was unheard of.

Olive was also given clan nicknames, alternately called "Aliutman," "Ali," "Olivino," or "Oach." According to a Mohave tribesman named Llewelyn Barrackman, these nicknames indicated that she was fully assimilated and adopted into the Mohave tribe. However, there were conflicting reports about Olive and Mary Ann's time with the Mohave tribe. Some say Olive's nickname "Spantsa" meant "rotten womb," which suggested Olive was sexually active during her time in the tribe, but that's not necessarily the case. It's also possible she was menstruating when she arrived at the Mohave camp, or they considered a white girl racially unhygienic.

However, as discussed earlier, the Mohaves embraced promiscuity and were very open and free when it came to sex. If Olive was involved sexually with Mohave men or women, she did not speak of such things when she was rescued. In addition, the Mohaves were fearful of having sex outside of their race, because they thought they would get sick or die. Therefore, sex between a white woman and a Mohave probably did not occur. That being said, if she was truly adopted into the tribe, as evidenced by her markings, she was also probably adopted into their race and, in turn, deemed acceptable for sex. Therefore, her nickname could have meant that Olive liked having sex so much with the Mohaves that she was sore and smelled rotten. Some historians, however, argued that nickname had numerous meanings, such as unquenchable thirst. No matter what the nicknames meant, they signified that Olive was accepted into the Mohave culture.

While the markings signified being welcomed into the tribal custom, Oatman later claimed in a book written by Reverend Royal B. Stratton that she was tattooed to signify that she was a slave. In the book, Olive claimed that both she and Mary Ann protested when the Mohave shamans first recommended tattoos. One might assume they objected because they were afraid of pain, but they more than likely already observed the process on others and noted it was not painful.

However, this is contradictory to Mohave custom; that is, the Mohave tradition states that the marks tattooed on the Oatman girls were only given to individuals who were properly assimilated into the tribe, not slaves. In addition, the precision and evenness of the facial markings show there was not a struggle, and Olive willingly submitted. Tattoos were supposed to protect the Mohaves after death and allow them to be recognized by their ancestors. The tribal members did not care if slaves were recognized in the land of the dead, so they did not routinely tattoo slaves.

Arrival Back to Civilization and Later Life

Olive Oatman assumed that she would spend the rest of her life with the Mohaves along the Colorado River. By the beginning of 1856 when Olive was an 18-year-old woman, she dressed in Mohave skirts, spoke the Mohave language, and answered others who used her Mohave names. Her skin turned brown due to constant exposure to the sun, which made her resemble her Mohave family more than ever. Over the years she was transformed from Olive Oatman, a white girl from a pioneer family, to a dark-skinned Mohave woman.

When Olive was 19, a Yuma Indian named Francisco arrived with a message: the post commander of Fort Yuma requested her return. Francisco was part of the Quechan tribe, a group of Indians that lived near the post. The Quechans were the tribe discussed earlier who scalped John Glanton and killed 15 men after they seized the Quechan's ferry service. They were California Indians who lived along the Colorado River. Most contemporary Quechan live on the Fort Yuma-Quechan Reservation near Yuma, Arizona, west of the Colorado River. According to Olive, she was told that Francisco came to "try and get me away to the whites".

Undoubtedly, Olive wondered how they learned she was alive. Rumors spread that a white girl lived with the tribe. As noted in Stratton's book, she first thought it was a trick to "deceive and excite" her, but then she realized the validity of the information she was told. One of the sub-chiefs verified that a Yuma Indian named Francisco was on his way with orders to immediately release Olive and return her to Fort Yuma.

At this point, European communities learned the impossible—white women lived among the Mohaves about 400 miles away from Fort Yuma. A messenger was sent to the tribe and requested that Olive be released. At first, the Mohave tribe fought the request to return Olive to Western society. They denied that Olive was white, although some voiced their affection for Olive, and others simply feared the repercussions for keeping her so long. Francisco vacated the area and went to homes of other nearby Mohaves before he returned for a second attempt at negotiation. The second time the messenger came with items to trade, including blankets and a white horse. But it was probably the threats that changed the Mohaves' minds, as he let them know the whites were set to destroy the Mohaves if they did not return Olive Oatman.

After negotiations from both sides, in which Olive participated, she was finally permitted to travel to Camp Yuma (formally named Fort Yuma) in February 1856. She was a captive of the Native Americans for five long years. A man named Mr. Henry Grinnell, a private citizen who worked as a mechanic at the fort, offered a ransom for Olive. Irish-born writer, artist, and government agent, John Ross Browne wrote about the Oatman massacre in 1871 and noted that Grinnell was "the only person who took interest in the matter" and who "from 1853 up to the date of the rescue never ceased to exert his energies to the end". Browne also recognized that Olive's return from the Mohaves was achieved because of the actions of Grinnell. Olive was escorted by Topeka, the daughter of the tribe leader who originally fought to save her from the Yavapais, on a 20-day journey to Fort Yuma.

Some claimed that Olive requested Western style clothing when she arrived at Camp Yuma, while others asserted that Olive was escorted by Mohaves to Camp Yuma after a man ran ahead and returned with a calico dress so she could return to her people properly clothed. Still another version stated she received Western clothing from the wife of an army officer, because she was only wearing a traditional Mohave skirt and no top. Regardless of the circumstances which surrounded her return, people were elated and cheered.

A few days later she received some incredible news—her brother was alive. All this time Olive Oatman thought her entire family was slaughtered, but Lorenzo survived the attack. After he escaped the massacre he searched tirelessly for Olive and Mary Ann. He was too late to save his younger sister, but Olive was returned safely after five years.

Mary Ann was always a sickly and frail child, and the years with the Native Americans took their toll on her weak body. In the mid-1800s a drought hit the region where the Mohaves lived. The result was a terrible deficiency in food supplies for the tribe. In 1853 Mary Ann was continuously sick throughout the summer months, and the Mohaves knew she was on borrowed time. Olive spent days looking for blackbird eggs so her sister could eat some much-needed protein, but it was too late. Many believed that Mary Ann, along with many Mohaves, died of starvation in 1855 or 1856. Olive said her sister's last words to her were, "I am willing to die. O, I shall be so much better off there!".

Olive described the scene surrounding Mary Ann as she took her last breath. Mary Ann never knew that her older brother was still alive and continued to search for her. She was about 10 or 11 at the time of her death, while Olive was around 19. Olive was saved from the same fate only because Aespaneo, the wife of tribe leader Espaniole, provided food to nourish her during the trying time. Espaniole helped make preparations to burn the body of Mary Ann, but instead it was decided that she have a proper burial. Olive chose a spot for her sister's eternal rest by a garden she had planted, and she was gently lowered into a grave. Olive mourned "the remains of my last, my only sister, and closed her last resting-place with the sand".

Olive Oatman went from unknown daughter of a pioneer family, to Indian captive, to Indian family member, to celebrity. In late 1864 she met a 34-year-old man while lecturing about her life at the Farmington church in Michigan. The man was

John Brant Fairchild. He radically affected the rest of Olive Oatman's life. Olive was introduced to Fairchild and his three sisters. In November 1865 Olive married the cattleman in Rochester, Monroe, New York.

Fairchild was born in January 1830 in New York and moved to Michigan with his family when he was a boy. In 1849 he traveled alone to California. During one of these trips he had his own tragic experience with the Apaches. Fairchild's brother, Rodney, died as the result of an attack in 1854 during a cattle drive.

The couple never had children of their own, but they adopted a baby girl named Mary Elizabeth, in honor of their mothers. Mary Elizabeth's nickname was "Mamie," and she was a symbol of Olive Oatman Fairchild's charity work with the local orphanage. The couple settled in Sherman, Texas to start their new life. Fairchild was a prosperous businessman, while his wife became what was known as the town's "Veiled Lady." The story about Olive became convoluted based on the writings of two men. There are many accounts of Olive Oatman's time with the Mohaves that contradict one another. The first one, which painted the Mohaves in a negative light through direct quotes from Olive Oatman herself, was written by Reverend Royal B. Stratton. Stratton wrote Olive's story in a fictional sense to portray intrigue, sex, and murder. Stratton wove a story of a young white pioneer woman who lived with the Mohaves against her will. A man by the name of A. L. Kroeber painted a much different picture in an academic journal. His accounts showed the Mohaves as a loving and caring tribe that took Olive in out of sheer kindness and compassion. In Kroeber's view the Mohaves saved Olive and her sister, and Olive was eternally grateful.

Account 1 – Reverend Royal B. Stratton

The story of Olive Oatman quickly spread across America, making her a celebrity. This popularity prompted a Methodist reverend named Royal B. Stratton to include Olive's story when he co-wrote the best-selling 1857 biography, *Life Among the Indians*. The book sold 30,000 copies. It detailed how her captors deprived Olive of the Mormon faith she practiced for the first 14 years of her life and, instead, lived among the Mohave Indians who he called "degraded bipeds". His book also made some disturbing claims that Olive and Mary Ann were, indeed, captives of the Mohave tribe and lived with them only because they feared to leave them. Stratton's book made negative claims about the famous chin markings. He asserted that Olive did not want them, because she knew they would make her an outsider with the whites if she was ever saved.

There were many experiences that made people question Stratton's depiction of the Oatman sisters' time with the

Mohaves. For example, when a large group of whites visited the Mohaves while Olive and Mary Ann were "held captive" in 1854, why did Olive refrain from making any contact with them? They were white railroad surveyors who spent nearly a week in the Mohave Valley socializing and trading with the Mohave tribe. That was ample time to tell the white men who she really was, Olive Oatman, daughter of the deceased Royce and Mary Ann Oatman from Illinois. Was she in fear for her life if she revealed that fact? And years later, when Olive was re-assimilated into white society, why did she meet with a Mohave leader named Irataba in New York City to reminisce about their times together? Would meeting with him have been too painful if she was a captive against her will? Finally, why did she always keep a jar of hazelnuts, a Mohave staple, with her as a reminder of her life as a Mohave? Some believe she did not reveal herself because she had no idea her brother was alive. Therefore, she thought she had no family besides the Mohaves, who had taken her in and showed affection for her.

Olive and her brother accompanied Stratton on a cross-country book tour. Olive was the main attraction due to the spectacle of being the first recorded American white woman tattooed by Native Americans. Not only were her tattoos a point of curiosity, but she was one of the first female public speakers when the concept of feminism was developed. The first wave of feminism started in 1850 with the pursuit of legal equal rights for women. Although feminism hit its peak between 1890 and 1920, the mid-1800s were the beginning of a shift in political rights and gender equality. Olive never claimed to be part of this feminist movement, but many people in America became aware of her shortly after the July 1848 Seneca Falls Convention. This was the first women's rights convention, which attracted widespread attention. Olive's notoriety as a female public speaker and heroine soon followed.

Stratton's book painted the Mohaves in an unfavorable light, but Olive was clear about their treatment. She denied rumors that she was sexually mistreated when she lived with the tribe. Olive was quoted in the book as stating that "to the honor of these savages let it be said, they never offered the least unchaste abuse to me". Royalties from the best seller allowed Olive and Lorenzo to attend the private Methodist-affiliated college, University of the Pacific. That being said, Olive never reached out to Stratton once she got married. Her husband burned all of the copies they had of Stratton's book, and Olive ceased her life as a public speaker. In fact, the Fairchilds did not invite Stratton to their wedding. Reverend Royal B. Stratton was institutionalized and died on January 24, 1875 at the age of 47 or 48.

Sales for the book, the *Captivity of the Oatman Girls*, continued to soar. The first print run was a measly 3,000 copies but climbed to 14,000. This was followed with 6,000 additional copies printed. By 1859 another 5,000 copies were released. The book already had two co-publishers, Carlton and Porter from New York and Ingham and Bragg from Cleveland, Ohio. Once the total printed copies of the book equaled 24,000, a third co-publisher named J. H. Seeley of Potsdam, New York, was added to the title page. The final printing of the *Captivity of the Oatman Girls* totaled a remarkable 27,000 books. The text was reprinted in 1983 by the University of Nebraska Press and then again in 1944 by Dover Publications. These impressive sales turned Olive Oatman into a celebrity and allowed her to make a living as a female public speaker and lecturer.

Account 2 – A. L. Kroeber

During the period of Olive Oatman's life with the Mohaves, the tribe had no written language. Stratton's story about the despicable treatment Olive received from the tribe was contradicted when an anthropologist named A. L. Kroeber interviewed a Mohave in 1903 who knew Olive. Kroeber was an American cultural anthropologist with an impressive résumé. He was awarded the first doctorate in anthropology from Columbia University and studied under the German pioneer of modern anthropology, Franz Boas. He was also known for his important work collecting cultural data on the western tribes of the Native Americans. Finally, Kroeber was a member of the Anthropology Department of the University of California, Berkeley.

Kroeber wrote a journal article about Oatman's time in captivity and further contradicted Stratton's findings when he published Olive's first interview with Martin Burke, the military commander who recovered her from the Mohaves. Her own accounts sounded like she was comfortable living with the Mohaves and did not want to leave her new home. Kroeber wrote in the *California Historical Society Quarterly:* "The Mohaves always told her she could go to the white settlements when she pleased but they dared not go with her, fearing they might be punished for having kept a white woman so long among them, nor did they dare to let it be known that she was among them". Kroeber also questioned why, when Lieutenant Amiel Whipple led the Pacific Railroad exploration directly through the Mohave Valley, she did not make any sign that she was a white captive. Why didn't Olive tell Lieutenant Whipple of her fate? Kroeber specifically asked, "was she in hiding voluntarily or by force?".

One of the tribal elders, Llewellyn Barrackman, was quoted as saying that they "felt sorry for her" and "we have a feeling for people". Barrackman was a long-time respected Mohave leader, a well-known force in Indian politics, and served on many private, state, and national boards and commissions. His word was respected until his death on May 21, 2006. He was also the tribal leader who insisted that Olive chose to be tattooed He asserted that the Mohave tribe never forced tattoos on anyone.

A childhood friend of Olive's named Susan Thompson, whom Olive again befriended in her later years, said she believed Olive grieved her Mohave husband and two children. However, Barrackman said she did not marry a Mohave or bear children: "She never married...It never was told. If it was we would all know". He also explained that if Olive had children with a Mohave man, they would have definitely stood out due to their coloring and features. It was not possible to document, however, whether Olive Oatman married a Mohave or not, since the tribe never had formal ceremonies or marriage certificates as evidence. If a Mohave man married a Mohave woman, they simply lived together. If a Mohave man divorced a Mohave woman, one of them moved out. If the couple had any children after the "divorce," they lived with their mother. Courting was simple. A boy and girl met at a party (feast), talked for a while, and had sex. If they stayed together, they were married. Unlike the Mormons, polygamy was rare and frowned upon. Adultery, however, was customary and accepted, although it sometimes created conflict between the women. It remained unclear whether Olive Oatman participated in such practices.

THE DEATH AND LEGACY OF OLIVE OATMAN

Olive Oatman Fairchild died of a heart attack on March 21, 1903 at the age of 65. She outlived her brother by two years. Lorenzo died on October 8, 1901. Olive's husband died on April 25, 1907. Her final resting place is West Hill Cemetery in Sherman, Texas. The name Olive Oatman, however, lived on in American history. In fact, the name Olive Oatman was bestowed on many girls born in the late 1850s and early 1860s.

Since her death, Olive's story has been recreated in numerous articles, books, plays, and works of art. Stories about her are now the stuff of legend. There is a town that bears her family name, Oatman, Arizona. Named in honor of Olive's life, struggles, and triumphs, the town is located in the Black Mountains of Mohave County. The town began as a small mining camp after two prospectors found $10 million in gold in 1915, which caused the population to swell to more than 3,500 in a year.

It was rumored that the famous actors Clark Gable and Carole Lombard spent their honeymoon in an Oatman hotel after their 1939 wedding in Kingman, Arizona. It was later revealed, however, that the famous couple returned to Los Angeles after their wedding and honeymooned in Baja, California. By the 1960s the town that bore Olive's name was all but abandoned, but her legacy lives on. For example, American novelist, short story writer, and screenwriter Elmore Leonard based his 1982 short story *The Tonto Woman* and his 1998 book *The Tonto Woman and Other Stories* on Oatman. Other books based on Olive's life include the 1872 Maria Amparo Ruiz de Burton book *Who Would Have Thought It?*, Elizabeth Grayson's 1997 *So Wide the Sky*, Wendy Lawton's 2003 book called *Ransom's Mark*, and the 2009 book written by Margo Mifflin, *The Blue Tattoo: The Life of Olive Oatman*.

Olive Oatman's name also appeared in an episode of the television series *The Ghost Inside My Child: The Wild West and Tribal Quest*, when a family claimed their daughter Olivia was the reincarnation of Olive Oatman. In the television show called *Death Valley Days*, Shary Marshall played Olive Oatman in a 1965 episode that also starred former actor turned United States President Ronald Reagan as Lieutenant Colonel Burke. Olive has been the subject of several children's books. More recently, a character in the AMC television series *Hell on Wheels* named Eva Oakes is loosely based on the life of Olive Oatman.

Her legacy lives on in tourist stops in Arizona, including Olive City, Oatman Mountain, Oatman Flat, and Oatman Flat

Station. Two individuals named Deborah and Jon Lawrence took a tour of the Oatman sites across the Midwest and documented their trip in the publication *Desert Tracks* in December 2005. They visited La Harpe, which had a small display of the Oatman family and a plaque in memory of Royce Oatman and his family, Morrison, east of the Mississippi River, and the Abbott farm. Who owns the Abbott farm? Ed Abbott, the great-grandson of Asa and Sarah Sperry Abbott. They also have a picture of Lorenzo Oatman's grave in Red Cloud, Nebraska.

Olive Oatman became an iconic figure in America's Western history, as she changed from a normal 14-year-old white Mormon girl to Native American Mohave with a tattooed chin. It was clear that Olive Oatman was a captive slave to the Yavapais. Was she a captive of the Mohaves, or did she want to stay with them and live her life as one of their own? In the end, did she consider herself white or Mohave? Those questions may never be answered, as Olive Oatman straddled the line of those two distinctive lives. Her life was portrayed much differently in the media. Stratton developed a fictional account of Olive's captivity, a parable of a damsel in distress. Kroeber, on the other hand, documented in an academic journal article a much different story, one of a loving Mohave family. Since Olive Oatman is no longer here to tell us, the truth of her story remains unknown.

In the end, Olive Oatman is remembered as the first white woman in America to be tattooed, and those unique and distinguishing blue lines across her chin forever symbolized her story, that of a white woman who straddled two very different worlds.

Printed in Great Britain
by Amazon